Mirror Sand

AN ANTHOLOGY
OF RUSSIAN SHORT POEMS
IN ENGLISH TRANSLATION

Mirror Sand

EDITED
AND
TRANSLATED
BY
ANATOLY
KUDRYAVITSKY

MIRROR SAND

An Anthology of Russian Short Poems in English Translation

Introduction copyright © Anatoly Kudryavitsky, 2018

English translations © Anatoly Kudryavitsky, 2006, 2018

Original Russian-language poems © their individual authors, 2018

This collection copyright © Glagoslav Publications, 2018

Front cover image © Jassemine Darouiech, 2018

Cover and layout design by Max Mendor

www.glagoslav.com

ISBN: 978-1-911414-72-8

A catalogue record for this book is available from the British Library

This book is in copyright. No part of this publication may be reproduced, stored in a retrieval system or transmitted in any form or by any means without the prior permission in writing of the publisher, nor be otherwise circulated in any form of binding or cover other than that in which it is published without a similar condition, including this condition, being imposed on the subsequent purchaser.

Acknowledgements

Grateful acknowledgement is made to the editors of the following, in which a number of these translations, or versions of them, originally appeared:

Hayden's Ferry Review, Cyphers, Das Gedicht, Poetry Ireland Review, The SHOp, Shot Glass Journal, SurVision, Public Pool, Four Centuries, World Poetry Almanac (Ulaanbaatar, Mongolia), *A Night in the Nabokov Hotel* anthology (Dedalus Press, 2006).

Some of these poems, in English translation, were first broadcast on RTÉ Radio 1.

Every effort has been made to trace the holders of the copyright to the works by Vladimir Burich, Mikhail Finerman and Arkady Tyurin, and to obtain permissions to reproduce their works. Please do get in touch with any enquiries or any information relating to their poems or the rights holders.

Contents

Acknowledgements 5

Introduction 13

Геннадий Айги / Gennady Aigi 19
    Тишина снега / The Silence of Snow 20
    Из цикла «Тишина» / Hush 22
    Дождь / The Rain 24
    Метель в окне / Snowstorm in My Window 26
    Путь / Our Way 28

Иван Ахметьев / Ivan Akhmetiev 31
    «Радость…» / The Challenge 32
    «пауза…» / A Pause 34
    «люди писали…» / Writing 36
    «когда я жду…» / Waiting 38
    «больше всего увидишь…» / Observation 40

Маргарита Аль / Margarita Al 43
    «скоро я стану гномом…» / Desire 44
    «из вечности в мгновенья вплетены…» / Wings 46
    «поэт…» / The Poet 48
    Зверь ещё не родился – но он уже зверь /
    The Beast Hasn't Been Born Yet – but It Already Is a Beast . . . 50
    Фарфоровое утро / A Porcelain Morning 52

Мария Алехина / Maria Alekhina 55
    «Кое-что из области удивлений…» / Pushkin Square 56
    «сырая белая комната сдержала три вопля…» / The Room . . 58

    «Следствие – страх...» / Prescience 60

    «Я совсем со временем...» / Time 62

    «ярость овцы на концах витков её шерсти...» / Simple Life . . 64

Геннадий Алексеев / Gennady Alexeyev . . 67

    Каждое утро / Every Morning 68

    Мои похороны / My Funeral 70

    Цветы / Flowers 72

    Стихи о том, как плохо быть человеком /
    A Poem About the Disadvantages of Being Human 74

    «Хочется, хочется...» / What I Want 76

Владимир Аристов / Vladimir Aristov . . . 79

    Из цикла «Московские мгновенные встречи» /
    From "Accidentally Met in Moscow" 80

    Поверхность китайского зеркала /
    The Surface of the Chinese Mirror 82

    «О дай мне жалости к дракону...» / The Dragon 84

    «Умнее мы уже не будем...» / For A.U. 86

    Инфернальные повторения / Infernal Repetitions 88

Сергей Бирюков / Sergey Biryukov 91

    «все меняется...» / Everything Changes 92

    «Тень...» / Who's Good? 94

    «вы так же встаете...» / Beastmen 96

    В скрипичном ключе / The Treble Clef 98

    Новые сведения о Петрарке и Лауре /
    News of Petrarch and Laura 100

Владимир Бурич / Vladimir Burich 103

    Я заглянул к себе ночью в окно /
    At Night I Looked into My Room Through the Window . . . 104

    «Так и не смог доесть...» / Half Past Seventies 106

    «Отцветут...» / What Will Remain 108

    Германия-1984 / Germany, 1984 110

    «На бульваре…» / On the Boulevard 112

Владимир Эрль / Vladimir Earle 115
    «Я в осень вошел, как во взгляд…» / Autumn 116
    «Преграда сна…» / The Barrier of Sleep 118
    «Когда люди имеют мнения…» / Opinions 120
    Эвридика / Eurydice 122
    «О!..» / Under Water 124

Михаил Файнерман / Mikhail Finerman 127
    «Касаясь...» / Touching 128
    «Как жёсткая зелень…» / Yearning 130
    «Свет предосенний редок…» / Name 132
    «Звери не хоронят своих мертвецов…» / Winter . . . 134
    «очутиться одному, на ветру…» / To Find Yourself . . 136

Руслан Галимов / Ruslan Galimov 139
    Прогноз / Forecast 140
    «Я долго был уверен…» / In General, She Was Right . . 142
    «Прекрасно общаясь…» / Agreeability 144
    «Я думал – это ГРОМ!..» / What Can Man Think About? . . 146
    «Сегодня думал я о смерти…» / Today 148

Татьяна Грауз / Tatyana Grauz 151
    Утренний сон / Morning Dream 152
    «в свете июля зелень паслёна…» / July's Light 154
    «неба-житель-бабочка…» / Butterfly 156
    Неяркое солнце / Soft Sun 158
    Апрель-голубка / April-Dove 160

Дмитрий Григорьев / Dmitry Grigoriev 163
    «Во тьме ты светишься…» / Night 164
    «Положи мои слова на землю…» / Words 166
    «Ночью…» / Shades of Night 168

«Мне говорили…» / Not Rubbish	170
«Рыбаки возвращаются без улова…» / Fishermen	172

Елена Кацюба / Elena Katsuba … 175

Свеча / Candle	176
«Дождь смотрит на бабочку сквозь стекло…» / Butterfly and the Rain	178
Вариант / An Apocryphal Story	180
На свалке заменимых нет! / There's Nothing Replaceable in the Dump!	182
«Жизнь сложена из лепестков розы…» / The Rose Garden	184

Константин Кедров / Konstantin Kedrov … 187

Иероглиф Бога / Hieroglyph for God	188
Аэроэра / Aero Era	190
Лодка / Keel	192
Свирель / Reed Pipe	194
Крылья / Wings	196

Игорь Холин / Igor Kholin … 199

«Камера…» / Cramer's Camera	200
«Если ты одинок…» / Poem for Edmund Iodkovsky	202
Из военного цикла / From "The War River"	204
«Ни звезды…» / Common Grave	206
«Одни говорят…» / Truths	208

Виктор Кривулин / Viktor Krivulin … 211

Рысь / Lynx	212
Пока мы изобретали рай / While We Invented Paradise	214
Книги и люди / Books and Men	216
Над гранитной фабрикой / Over the Granite Factory	218
Финал / The End	220

Анатолий Кудрявицкий / Anatoly Kudryavitsky … 223

Камерная музыка / Chamber Music	224

Бунин. Портрет с отсутствием объекта /
Bunin: Portrait with the Person Missing 226

Иуда / Judas 228

Незримое кино / The Invisible Cinema 230

Гибель MH-17 / The Shooting Down of MH17 232

Александр Макаров-Кротков / Alexander Makarov-Krotkov . . . 235

«хорошо выпить водки…» / For K. 236

«холодно-свинцовая масса…» / On the Quays . . . 238

«тихо так воет собачка…» / The Doggy. 240

Стокгольм / Stockholm 242

Джеймс Джойс глазами советского читателя /
A Soviet Reader's Remark on James Joyce 244

Арво Метс / Arvo Mets 247

«Поэт стоит в очереди за вермишелью…» / The Poet . . . 248

«Исчезаю в весне…» / Absentee 250

«Молодые девушки…» / Resemblance 252

«Безденежный человек…» / Penniless Man 254

«Этот странный обычай…» / Names 256

Юрий Милорава / Yuri Milorava 259

«единый…» / Untitled 1 260

«шоссе…» / Untitled 2 262

«тайный винт…» / Untitled 3 264

«ввинчена…» / Untitled 4 266

«бытие…» / Untitled 5 268

Всеволод Некрасов / Vsevolod Nekrasov 271

«Свобода есть…» / Freedom 272

«Молчу…» / Untitled-1 274

«надо же…» / Untitled-2 276

«Стой…» / Pride 278

«Не люблю…» / Love 280

Ры Никонова / Rea Nikonova 283
  «Кареты в белом...» / Simple 284
  «Все идиоты в этом мире идиотов...» /
  The World of Idiots 286
  Анти-новелла / Anti-Novella 288
  «Когда помру...» / Foretaste 290
  «Россия с иссneженным зубром...» / Russia 292

Генрих Сапгир / Genrikh Sapgir 295
  Роща / Grove 296
  «Говорили...» / New in Town 298
  «Красные портьеры...» / Business Trip 300
  Изречение / A Proverb 302
  «Тс-с...» / Sounds of Silence 304

Ян Сатуновский / Ian Satunovsky 307
  «В век сплошной электрификации...» /
  Changing the Bulb 308
  «Экспрессионизм-сионизм....» / If They So Desire . . 310
  «Ребенок рисунка...» / Almost by Mistake 312
  «...а, впрочем...» / Writing 314
  «Я Мойша з Бердычева...» / A Bloody Yid 316

Ася Шнейдерман / Asya Shneiderman 319
  «Не писать стихи, а слышать...» / Poetry 320
  «Разве башня из камня...» / The Tower 322
  «Город влажный лежал под нами...» / The City . . . 324
  «Друзья приходят в наш дом...» / Poem for Lena Zhukova . 326
  «Особенно в мире...» / Especially in this Kind of World . 328

Михаил Соковнин / Mikhail Sokovnin 331
  «Вот вам и чудо...» / Fantasy 332
  Лесовик / Woodsman 334
  «Самовар...» / Samovar 336

«Небо серое-серое…» / A Northern Song 338
«Заброшенные истины…» / Untitled 340

Сергей Стратановский / Sergey Stratanovsky 343
«Ночью, в Набоков-отеле…» / In the Nabokov Hotel 344
Акула-кунсткамера / A Shark as a Cabinet of Curiosities . . . 346
Левиафан / Leviathan 348
Башня-библиотека / The Library Tower 350
Апокриф / An Apocryphal Story 352

Аркадий Тюрин / Arkady Tyurin 355
Неразрывность / Inseparability 356
Неосторожно… / It Is Careless of You … 358
«Все отражает, не унося…» / Time and the River 360
«Был ей другом…» / She 362
«Запущен…» / Garden 364

Алина Витухновская / Alina Vitukhnovskaya 367
На ощупь / By Touch 368
Ваш хаос / Your Chaos 370
Ноль / Zero 372
Собака Павлова / Pavlov's Dog 374
Ева Браунинг / Eva Browning 376

Introduction

A saying has it that Russia produces more than it can consume locally. Should this refer to Russian poetry? Western readers are well acquainted with poetry written in that country over the last three centuries, from Alexander Pushkin to Anna Akhmatova, mostly through translations. Some other Russian poets, including Vladimir Nabokov and Joseph Brodsky, felt at home at writing in English. This book offers an opportunity to hear a few newer voices.

As Vladimir Nabokov once put it, "Literature belongs to the department of specific words and images rather than to the department of general ideas." Unfortunately, the general idea in Communist Russia was to encourage and publish only those writers who supported and even glorified the regime. It was Government policy, especially strict after the last world war. It is inconceivable now that any European poet could write a paean for the President of the European Council, but we have to bear in mind that in Communist Russia, even in the 1980s, this sort of poetry was a commonplace. Other poets ran the risk of being treated with suspicion by each and every literary vigilante. Should we be surprised by Marina Tsvetayeva's line: "All the poets are Jews"?

"After Pasternak, Russian poetry sustained a pause," the late Genrikh Sapgir used to say. It was destined to be a long pause. In fact, the generation of Russian writers that emerged in the early 60s grew up reading and studying in college Russian poetry from the 1920s. Some of them were particularly inspired by Boris Pasternak and Osip Mandelstam, others by Velimir Khlebnikov and other Russian Futurist poets. What appeared in Soviet "fat magazines" in those times were, to quote Anna Akhmatova, "rhymed editorials", or otherwise third-rate imitations of Symbolist poetry from the late nineteenth century.

In these circumstances some Russian poets chose to refrain from publishing anything openly, while others were banned from publishing. Writing "into the table" became customary for them. Many of them explored the possibilities of so-called "open poetry". By stripping their pieces down to a most basic expression, and outlawing most literary devices or even emotional colouring, they focused their attention on individual words, or even on fragments of those words and sound units from them. This style was later defined as minimalism. One can trace the sources of modern-day minimalist texts to Dadaist, Surrealist, Concrete and even Zen poetry, and it definitely displays parallels to the visual arts. Minimalist poets focused on bare words or phrases, sometimes rearranging them on the page so that their most basic and individual properties disclosed something unexpected about themselves.

The work of these poets wasn't minimalist in the sense that they had little to say; quite the contrary, it captured the frustration, suppressed ambitions and hidden energy of several generations of Russian people. As Vassily Kandinsky once put it, "Even absolute silence is a loud speech." Joseph Brodsky in one of his lectures compared Mark Strand and Charles Simic, well-established American "poets of silence", as he called them, to "unofficial" Russian poets who had to dwell in silence, due to having no other literary space. Rea Nikonova, a poet from the South of Russia, even produced a catalogue of different kinds of silence. She knew very well what she was talking about as she first lived in Yeysk, a small Russian town on coast of the Azov Sea – and then on the other shores of exile, in Germany, until her untimely death.

In the 1960s and 1970s, Genrikh Sapgir, Vsevolod Nekrasov and Igor Kholin were the most prominent among the Moscow writers that came to be associated with the now well-known Lianozovo group. These poets sought out new models and positions, and exploited the possibilities of inserting common speech directly into their texts. Each of them had a Dostoyevskian eye for everyday Russian life, which made their work immediately accessible. No wonder that they at once found themselves uncomfortable with authority and orthodoxy, and also with the authorities and the Orthodox Church, suppressed under the Communists but still powerful, as far as the minds of the Russians were concerned. These were real rebels, unlike a few other Russian poets who enjoyed virtual pop-star status, unthinkable if transposed to other parts of Europe. In reality, the latter were far from any sort of protest against Soviet totalitarianism and therefore could not be regarded as anything else but naughty children of the regime.

The idea of a cultural centre was particularly dispiriting for those who were geographically based far from Moscow and therefore felt marginalised. Gennady Aigi and Arvo Mets are typical of the rise of poets who settled down in the Russian capital and preferred to write in Russian rather than in their mother tongues, in this case respectively Chuvash and Estonian. The sources of their poetry were different; no wonder that their verse sounded so fresh and enriched the Russian language to such a great extent. Poems by Gennady Aigi are derived entirely from individual words and sometimes from single syllables and sounds. He created his own language, an independent and unique speech or, if you prefer, chant. Interestingly, both Gennady Aigi and Arvo Mets made a great deal of translations and so participated in an exchange of "poetic air" with other cultures.

Those who followed were quick to learn from the emotion of poems by Sapgir and other poets of Lianozovo and the variety of poetic forms elaborated by Aigi and Vsevolod Nekrasov. Sergey Biryukov born in the South of Russia inhabits approximately the same territory as Aigi, as does the younger-generation Moscow poet Tatyana Grauz, but they are both prone to experiment with syntax and language rather than with the available voices. Behind Biryukov stand the famous Russian Futurist poets, Mayakovsky, Khlebnikov and Kruchenykh.

In Moscow in the 1970s, there was also a "verlibrist" movement (from *vers libre,* i.e. free verse), a group of poets that included, among others, Vladimir Burich, Arkady Tyurin and the Tatar poet Ruslan Galimov. They experimented with shorter poetic forms; as short as those used by Arvo Mets, and occasionally managed to get some of their poems published, although the literary powers that be were not particularly keen on this kind of poetry preferring "ideologically safe" rhymed quatrains, which some Russians call "traditional", even though they were imported from French poetry about three centuries ago. In the 1990s, the "verlibrists" published a few warmly received anthologies of Russian free verse.

There were also predominantly minimalist Moscow poets, e.g. Mikhail Finerman and Ian Satunovsky; the former developing short-form sophisticated poetry in the traditions of Zen, and the latter keen on exploring the possibilities of incorporating direct speech in his texts. They often wrote even shorter pieces than those by "verlibrists", and their followers, Alexander Makarov-Krotkov and Ivan Akhmetiev, appreciated sparringness, too. Similarly to Vsevolod Nekrasov, they succeeded in dismantling traditional forms of irony and understatement. Finerman, Satunovsky and another Moscow poet of the 1970's, Mikhail Sokovnin, who wrote lyrical miniatures, as well as *predmetniki,* i.e. object-based poems, saw their work published only after Soviet imperial ambitions in ideology died a hard death, only to be revived far too soon amid the expanses of what at least some of them would inevitably see as an eager-to-expand Wasteland.

Of course, it was no surprise that magic realism became one of the main trends in Russian poetry. The great figures of Nikolai Gogol and Mikhail Bulgakov cast long shadows over Russian writing. In his essay, *Catastrophes in the Air,* Joseph Brodsky defined the way in which writers of that strain worked. He described the metamorphosis of Andrei Platonov, the prominent Russian magic realist of the early twentieth century, novelist and short story writer, in the following terms: "He tells the story about his own language, which turns out to be capable of generating a fictitious world, and then falls into dependence on it." The language used by most of the Russian magic realists has always been saturated with metaphors. Mandelstam was as much of a revolutionary as any Bolshevik, and Russian poetry could never be the same after his verse was published.

Poets of the Moscow-based Poetry Club mostly followed the customary metaphorical trend. One of them, Vladimir Aristov, was trying, quite successfully, to escape the negative inheritance of newer Russian poetry: its ironies and superficiality. Different realities and different times coincide in Aristov's verse, unmistakably "within a culture" – but also multicultural. It seems that one can occasionally trace foreign presences in work by some Russian poets: e.g. William Blake and Saint-John Perse in Genrikh Sapgir and T. S. Eliot in Vladimir Aristov. The author of these lines, one of the poets associated with the so-called DOOS group, must confess that in his green years he was much inspired by the work of such different poets as William Carlos Williams and Zbigniew Herbert.

The poets of the DOOS group founded by Konstantin Kedrov and Elena Katsuba in the early 1980s claimed that they invented meta-metaphors. True or not, their work is not merely aestheticism but also offers a critique of the bankrupt vocabularies of "official" Russian poetry – simply by suggesting newer and more interesting options for using the language. DOOS made experimental poetry attractive to the younger generations of poets who later joined the group, like Margarita Al.

The writing of Alina Vitukhnovskaya, who emerged in the 1990s, is energised by a tension between ironic social naturalism and ideological aspirations. She violently denounces any kind of violence, and ridicules complacency of the Establishment. Her poems, radically anarchic in their conception, are fairly sound and "well-built". Another protest voice in this book, the young Moscow poet and human rights activist Maria Alekhina of *Pussy Riot* fame, often describes reality's unusual features and sometimes gives it a surreal aura, as does the Russian-language Georgian poet Yuri Milorava, who lived in Moscow in the 1990s and is now based in Chicago. They both write poetry seeking to recreate the world of their visions.

Russia has always been a huge and bipolar country. The difference between Moscow and St. Petersburg poetry can make one feel that these two cities are located in different countries. The so-called New Leningrad School of Poetry that emerged in St. Petersburg at the beginning of the 1970s was extremely influential in the then seemingly invisible culture of the Russian literary underground. The group included the Nobel Prize winner Joseph Brodsky, as well as Sergey Stratanovsky and the late Viktor Krivulin and Elena Shvarts. Viktor Krivulin's obsession with Dante set him on a mental journey through the circles of some sort of hell, or "counterfeit Eden", which he found in his urban habitation, but also inside the minds of many of his countrymen. Sergey Stratanovsky is now perceived by many as the leading living St. Petersburg poet; he displays determination to remind us of the great cultural traditions of St. Petersburg, the former capital of Russia, and their deterioration under the Communists.

Incidentally, many St. Petersburg poets of the 1990s seemed to take after Brodsky who had been exiled in 1972; others developed pretty sophisticated poetry according to the good old canons. Gennady Alexeev was the first St. Petersburg poet ever to choose *vers libre* as his poetic device. His texts are quite recognisable as having their roots in his own emotional expressionism. He preserved a relatively unadulterated singleness in the first person, as did Vladimir Earle in his rather unusual melodious poems written in the 1970s. Younger St. Petersburg poets – notably Dmitri Grigoriev and Asya Shneiderman – rarely find it possible to locate a single self in their work. Dmitri Grigoriev often portrays urban blight and paranoia, while Asya Shneiderman derives inspiration from shades of the Cimmerian or even biblical past, seemingly quite distinct and pictorial in her inner sight.

The work collected here documents poetry in Russia responding to the challenges of the time by forging a radical new poetic, reconsidering writing techniques and language itself. Some of the poets represented in this book are long gone but some others have only just begun. Alongside the fellow poets of their generation, they are destined to shape the Russian poetry of the future. What they have achieved is considerable but they all have a great leap forward in them. In his essay *The Keening Muse*, Brodsky asserted: "Language is older than state, and prosody always survives history. In fact, it hardly needs history, all it needs is a poet." In Russia, we have always had a few!

Anatoly Kudryavitsky
Dublin, Ireland

Геннадий Айги
Gennady Aigi

Gennady Aigi (1934–2006) was born in the Chuvash Republic, and lived in Moscow. His translations of French poetry into the Chuvash language brought him recognition at the beginning of his career as a writer. However his unusual work was not welcomed in Russian periodicals and publishing houses. After perestroika, he published many critically acclaimed books of his poetry in Russian and Chuvash, as well as numerous essays and translations. His poems were translated into many languages. Without exaggeration, he was the most celebrated Russian poet of the time. A book of his poems in French translation entitled *Veronica's Notebook* was published in Paris in 1984. Peter France of Edinburgh published two books of his translations from Aigi into English, much appreciated. Aigi was awarded the Golden Wreath of Struga (Macedonia), the French Academy Translators' Award and the Andrey Belyi Prize for Poetry (1987). In 2000, he was awarded the first ever Boris Pasternak Prize for Poetry.

Тишина снега

без начала
как времени
ниоткуда они пребывают
без происхождения мирные
вольные не иметь и отдельное что-то и общее
не проявляя места и подобия
быть знаемыми иль возможными
о просто они и они пребывая
миром одним
тишиною

The Silence of Snow

without a beginning
as is in time
they arrive from nowhere
they have no background peaceful
free not to have something separate
or something in common
not revealing a place or a similarity
to be known, to be a possibility
oh they—and the other "they" too—are simply
dwelling in the same world
amid the silence

Из цикла «Тишина»

а те с того самого времени как начали
видеть свет божий
стали впервые теперь различать
черное от белого
и пришли в восторг и торопятся уже сообщить
вот это – белое
а это черное

Hush

…and some people have been trying
to tell the black from the white
since the very first moment
they saw the daylight…
they succeed at long last
and go into raptures and hasten
to bring to our notice: this is white
and that is black

Дождь

и моросит и утихает
как будто возится сама с собой "случайность"

(как "одаренность" годная
лишь для набросков жалких)

как будто "есть" "живет"

(в кругу – как я – ненужности)

The Rain

drizzles and subsides
as if "fortuity" is romping with itself

(just as a "talent"
capable only of middling sketches)

as if "it exists" really exists

(in the circle of uselessness –
exactly where I find myself)

Метель в окне

В.Я.

Метель в окне и стены комнаты
и затеряв меня давно во вьюге дом
рисунков на стенах собрание как в прятках
как в юности – в ее далекой свежести
когда (метель) окно: как тайну: ладила
свое: то там то здесь:
немного поправляя

Snowstorm in My Window

(For V.Y.)

a snowstorm in my window – and these walls
of my room – my house has long lost sight of me in a blizzard
the collection of drawings on the walls
playing hide-and-seek with me –
                     reminds me of how it used to be
in my youth in those days of freshness when it
                     (the snowstorm)
decorated my window building a mystery
                     and going into details
adjusting every little thing:
now here, now there

Путь

Когда нас никто не любит
начинаем
любить матерей

Когда нам никто не пишет
вспоминаем
старых друзей

И слова произносим уже лишь потому
что молчанье нам страшно
а движенья опасны

В конце же – в случайных запущенных парках
плачем от жалких труб
жалких оркестров

Our Way

When nobody likes us
we learn
how to love our mothers

When nobody writes to us
we call to mind
old friends

And we utter a few words – simply because
we're scared of silence
and deem any movement dangerous

And in the end we sob in a park overgrown
with shrubs as we hear the pitiable trumpets
of a pitiable brass band

Иван Ахметьев
Ivan Akhmetiev

Ivan Akhmetiev was born in Moscow in 1950. Educated at Moscow State University, where he studied physics, he began to write at the end of 1960s. Until 1989 only one of his poems was published in Russia. Since then many of his poems have appeared in literary magazines in Russia and abroad. Critics defined him as a minimalist and miniaturist. He has published four poetry collections entitled *Poems, only Poems* (1993), *Nine Years* (2001), *Amores: Poems 1966-2002* (2002) and *Never Mind It Will Turn Out All Right* (2011). Some of his miniatures have been translated into German and English.

* * *

радость
приходит нечаянно
наше дело –

найти для печали
предлог

The Challenge

joy
comes unexpectedly

the challenge is
to find an excuse
for sadness

* * *

пауза
которую я сделаю
прежде чем ответить
скажет вам больше

A Pause

if I make a pause
before I reply to the words of yours
the moment of silence
will be quite eloquent

* * *

люди писали
и в лагере
и в тюрьме
и в психушке
и где только не писали

главное
делать это незаметно

Writing

some people
would write in jail
in a labour camp
in an asylum

where have they not written!

the main thing is
to go unnoticed

* * *

когда я жду
я уже не жду
и как бы не нуждаюсь
дождаться

так и дожидаюсь

Waiting

when I am waiting
I am no longer waiting
I don't even need
to wait till it happens, indeed

this is the way I do the waiting

* * *

больше всего увидишь
если замрешь на одном месте
на зиму
лето
ночь
день
как старый чемодан на балконе

Observation

you will see more
if you stand motionless on the spot
for the whole winter
summer
night
day –
like an old trunk on the balcony

Маргарита Аль
Margarita Al

Margarita Al (pen name of Margarita Almuhametova) was born in 1959 in Alma-Aty, Kazakhstan, and now lives in Moscow. A poet, an artist and a graphic designer, she runs DOOS Books, which publishes *The PO Journal* and poetry books. She is a member of the DOOS group of poets and of the Academy of Zaum association of Futurist poets, and has published two collections of her poetry, *Stating the Denial* (with Konstantin Kedrov, 2009) and *Mirazhi Zn* (2014). Margarita Al was awarded the David Burliuk Prize for life-long commitment to experimental poetry.

* * *

скоро я стану гномом
всё выше
и гуще лес
я думала вырастить сад
вырастить сад
для Бога
но прежде взойдёт Звезда
в паутине теней бесконечности
я думала вырастить сад
где каждое дерево райское

Desire

I'll soon turn into a gnome
the forest thickens
grows higher
I thought about setting up a garden
for the Supreme Creator
but it can't be done until the star
rises among entangled shadows of infinity
I thought about setting up a garden
where every tree
is the tree of paradise

* * *

из вечности в мгновенья вплетены
невидимые взору крылья человека
как тени ангелов
взлетают в небо птицы
как тени птиц – следы в чужую жизнь
чем удивить могу я этот мир неповторимый
что может жизнь в бессмертие внести

Wings

invisible wings of the humans
hang down from eternity
woven into moments in time
resembling shadows of angels
birds soar into the sky like shadows of birds
or footprints leading into somebody's life
how can I can surprise this unrivalled world?
how can life contribute to immortality?

* * *

поэт
послушен слову своему
в нём не разрушен храм
мгновения
любить
не ведая того

The Poet

the poet
is true to his word
his inner temple of the moment
is intact
unknowingly
he is in love

Зверь ещё не родился – но он уже зверь

мысль когда-то была ребёнком
в этой купели крестили звёзды
мысль когда-то была небом
в этой купели крестили слово
слово когда-то мычали Боги
небо вскрывая корявым звуком
человек ещё не родился
но губы уже пели

The Beast Hasn't Been Born Yet – but It Already Is a Beast

once upon a time thought was a child
in this font the stars were baptised
once upon a time thought was a sky
in this font the word was baptised
the word was once mooed by the gods
as they opened up the sky with a gruff sound
a man hadn't been born yet
but a song already was on his lips

Фарфоровое утро

ещё туман сплавляют по реке
но свет уже готов нарушить тишину слепых зеркал
фарфоровое утро на столе

A Porcelain Morning

the fog is still being rafted down the river
but the light is ready to break the silence
    of the blind mirrors
a porcelain morning on the table

Мария Алехина
Maria Alekhina

Maria Alekhina was born in 1988 in Moscow. She is a graduate of the Institute of Journalism and Creative Writing in Moscow, a poet and a musician, one of the founding members of the band *Pussy Riot*, an environmental activist with Greenpeace Russia and a human rights activist. On August 17, 2012, she was convicted of "hooliganism motivated by religious hatred" for a performance in Moscow's Cathedral of Christ the Saviour and sentenced to two years' imprisonment. Amnesty International named her a prisoner of conscience due to "the severity of the response of the Russian authorities." Her collection titled *Poems and Essays* appeared in Moscow in 2012; she has also published a memoir, *Riot Days* (2017; an English translation is due from Allen Lane / Penguin Books). In 2013, she was nominated for the Politprosvet Journalism Award, and in 2014 was the recipient of The Hannah Arendt Prize for Political Thought.

* * *

Кое-что из области удивлений,
Метеоритного молотка. Такой
Город, состоящий из преступлений:
Не верится даже, что твой и мой.

Слева вешают надпись на красном,
Справа вешают красных, а я
С одной ноги на другую в напрасном
Снегу опускаю взгляд.

Рупор упругий, с выкриком спаренный,
Ленточки треплет в волосах,
И Пушкин на фоне, даром что каменный,
Получается как бы не при делах.

Pushkin Square

It comes as some kind of surprise,
some kind of meteor strike.
We dwell in a crime zone. I can't believe
this is your city, my city.

On my left, somebody hangs a red banner,
on my right, somebody hangs the reds. And I
shift from one foot to the other
making the snow squeak, looking down.

A megaphone shout-out
ruffles the ribbons in my hair.
In the background, the Pushkin statue,
a man of stone left on his own.

* * *

сырая белая комната сдержала три вопля
в тех местах остались обои
застывшими пузырями
пятнами синими на стене проступали
вниз стекали и под пол уходили
и когда в эту комнату мы заходили
то замолкали
и те кто любил уже не любили
за окном птицы уже не летали
только тени по белому потолку плыли
и сливались с нами

The Room

The damp white room held back three screams
wallpaper lingered there
as frozen bubbles
as blue patches that oozed through the wall
and then streamed down and under the floor
whenever we entered that room
we fell silent
and those who were in love fell out of love
out the window birds were no longer flying
only shadows drifted across the white ceiling
and merged with us

* * *

Следствие – страх.
О, что мы?
– Разбились о капли, о стены.
Явились ли после кому?
Только, Боже, тебе одному.

И храни мою руку,
Когда просо слов
Брошу
И предам сразу же – жди меня.

На набережной,
На берегу
Я от них убегу.

Prescience

Fear is the consequence.
What are we? We crashed
against water drops, against the walls.
And later, did we appear before anyone?
Only before God.

Steady my hand
as I sow the millet of words –
and instantly become a traitor.
Then – wait for me.

On a distant shore,
on a quay,
from them all I'll flee.

* * *

Я совсем со временем
я со всем – но пока
я со временем буду как все
рука разберёт в волосах пробор
горстку дроби в голову вложит
тёплый волной кожный покров
соберётся поверх
но позже
когда к ушам прирастут
раковины покоя
и тихое эхо прибоя
разгладит внутренний жгут

Time

I am totally with time
I am with everything – for the time being
but I'll eventually learn how to be like everyone else
my hand will part my hair
and lodge a handful of small shots inside my head
the wave of my warm skin
will cover it from above
but this will happen later
when my ears adhere
to the conch shells of calm
and the quiet echo of the surf
smoothens my inner wisp

* * *

ярость овцы на концах витков её шерсти
сверкает под круглой и жёлтой луной
ряд свежих дров поджидает верёвка и если
хозяин их свяжет то ляжет со мной
то звук кочерги, то ухвата плохая примета
забирается сырость по согретым ногам
гусеничным ползком, по лодыжкам коленкам
и выше взмывает в предрассветный туман

Simple Life

The rage of a sheep at the ends of its wool coils
sparkles under the round-shaped yellow moon
a row of freshly chopped logs is awaiting a rope and if
the owner ties them together he'll share the bed with me
the sound of a poker followed by the bad omen of an oven fork
dampness crawls up my warm legs
the way caterpillars crawl, from my ankles to my knees –
and then it soars into the predawn fog

Геннадий Алексеев
Gennady Alexeyev

Gennady Alexeyev (1932–1987) lived in St. Petersburg, and lectured on history of art at St. Petersburg University. He was the first to introduce *vers libre* (free-verse) in St. Petersburg. Writing in that style as early as 1953, he published his first poem in 1962, but had difficulty publishing poetry thereafter as it was deemed too "different". During his life time four collections of his poems appeared in Russia. Two more were published soon after his death, including *Me and the City* (1991). Two volumes of his *Collected Poems* were also published in St. Petersburg posthumously. Undoubtedly, he was one of the most important St. Petersburg poets of the second half of the last century; arguably, the most underestimated.

Каждое утро

Каждое утро,
когда я открываю глаза,
я вижу окно
и в окне – небо.

Каждое утро
оно напоминает мне о том,
что я не птица.

Every Morning

Every morning
I open my eyes
and see the window,
and in that window, the sky.

Every morning
it reminds me:
I'm not a bird.

Мои похороны

мои похороны были скромными
я шел за своим гробом один
с букетиком фиалок в руке
день был солнечным
на кладбище пели птицы
и могильщики были навеселе
потом я напился на своих поминках
плакал
и горланил дурацкие песни
я был доволен собой
потому что умер вовремя.

My Funeral

my funeral was modest
I walked alone behind my coffin
with a bouquet of violets in hand
it was a sunny day
birds were singing in the cemetery
and the gravediggers were plastered
later I got drunk at my funeral repast
I cried
and bawled stupid songs
I was pleased with myself
because I died at the right time.

Цветы

Цветы
пахнут похоронами
и любовью.
Но они
ни в чем не виноваты.
Иногда
ими осыпают негодяев,
иногда
их дарят круглым дурам,
иногда
их воруют на кладбище
и продают втридорога влюбленным.
Но цветы
ни в чем не виноваты.
Им не стыдно,
что Джордано Бруно
был сожжен на площади Цветов.

Flowers

Flowers
smell of funerals
and love.
But it's not their fault.

Sometimes people
shower flowers on rascals
or present them
to a stupid bit of skirt.

Sometimes you see flowers
stolen from gravestones
and then sold to pairs
of sweethearts
at an exorbitant price.
But it's not their fault.

Flowers are not embarrassed by the fact
that Giordano Bruno was burnt
on the Square of Flowers.

Стихи о том, как плохо быть человеком

Хорошо быть обезьяной,
и попугаем хорошо быть,
и крысой,
и комаром,
и амебой.

Плохо быть человеком:
все понимаешь.
Понимаешь,
что обезьяна – кривляка,
попугай – дурак,
крыса – злюка,
комар – кровопивец,
а амеба – полное ничтожество.

Это удручает.

A Poem About the Disadvantages of Being Human

It's good to be a monkey,
and equally good to be a parrot,
a rat,
a mosquito,
an amoeba.

It's not very good to be human:
you understand everything.
You can see
that the monkey is a poseur,
the parrot is a fool,
the rat is wicked,
the mosquito is a bloodsucker,
and the amoeba is a complete nonentity.

This is depressing.

* * *

Хочется, хочется...
мало ли чего хочется?

хочется сказать:
да будьте вы прокляты!
но я говорю:
да простит вас бог!

What I Want

I want, I want...
Who cares what I want?

I want to say:
Damn you all to hell! –
but what I say is,
God forgive you.

Владимир Аристов
Vladimir Aristov

Vladimir Aristov was born in 1950 in Moscow, where he still lives. Educated at Moscow Institute of Technology and Physics, he started writing poetry at the end of the 1970s. He was a member of the so-called Poetry Club circle, which included predominantly ironic poets. His poems, essays and short stories remained unpublished until the years of perestroika. Since then, ten critically acclaimed collections of his poetry, including *Moving Away from this Winter* (1992), *Private Follies of Things* (1997), *Names and Faces in the Metro* (2011), and *Open Backyards* (2016), appeared in Russia, as well as his novel, *The Witness's Prophecy* (2004). His short stories were published in *Zhuzhukiny Deti*, the anthology of Russian short stories and prose miniatures written in the second half of the last century (2000). His work has been translated into several European languages.

Из цикла «Московские мгновенные встречи»

(12 час. 48 мин., 26-сентября, Яузские ворота)

…встретился совершенно незнакомый человек
Несмотря на солнце, в капюшоне
Правой рукой опираясь на палку, шел наразмашку
В левой – с раскрытою книжкой в желтой обложке
Взгляд его был, как пароль
И в лице непрочитанные морщины.

From "Accidentally Met in Moscow"

(Yauza Gates, 26 September, 12.48pm)

... met a completely unknown man,
Hooded, despite the sunshine,
Walking sweepingly, right hand on a walking stick,
In the left, an open book with a yellow cover;
His look was like a password,
And his face had unread wrinkles.

Поверхность китайского зеркала

Можжевельник у озера?

Стена по горе промелькнула спиною дракона

Там дальше по стене
В нерастворимую бесконечность
Сносит ветер границу аммиака
По дикой тропке

Здесь между стёкол автобуса можно
Комикс жизни своей
Перевести в допотопную быль

Ведь на дне многоугольника
         Рисового болота
И жевательный автограф нейтрален
Но певучая немота – не монета...

The Surface of the Chinese Mirror

Juniper by the lake?

The wall flashed across the mountain as a dragon's back

Further down that wall
The wind blows the boundary of ammonia
Along the wild trail
Into an insoluble infinity

Here between the window panes of the bus
You can translate the comic book of your life
Into a true antediluvian story

After all, at the bottom of the polygonal
       Rice bog
Even the chewable autograph is neutral
But the melodious dumbness is not a coin...

* * *

О дай мне жалости к дракону,
Пока он спит,
И диктор шепчет равнодушным словом
Его дневную речь.
Покуда он не пробудился,
В глазах кровавые глубины не открылись.
Пока Георгий не пришел,
Свое копье не погрузил
В бессильный глаз.
Пока от боли дракон не стал столь человечным.
Дай мне успеть, покуда жив Георгий.
И диктор не способен в страхе
Летучей мыши сквозь себя полет сдержать
И в воздух словом отпускает.

The Dragon

O grant me pity for the Dragon
While he lies there fast asleep,
And a radio announcer whispers indifferently
The monster's daily speech.
Until the Dragon is awake
And blood-stained depths open in his eyes.
Until St. George arrives and drives his spear
Into the Dragon's feeble eye.
Until the monster, in great pain,
Becomes incredibly humane.

O give me time while St. George is still alive
And that announcer, frightened, is unable to prevent
A bat from flying through himself,
And so he utters words that instantly
Release it into the air.

***

А.Ю.

Умнее мы уже не будем,
И лучше мы уже не станем.
Фонарный свет лица ночного
Отцвел и в сад сошел за поездом вослед.

Я помню тот китайский парк.
Бордюры из камней, людская лень
Из кособоков облака над хижинами века.
Цемент плакучий и бензин бессильный.

Под вишнями и яблонями зимними в саду
Лишь проволока растет стальная.

For A.U.

We'll never be wiser than we are,
nor shall we improve.
The lantern light of a nocturnal face
has lost its bloom and retired to the garden.

I recall vividly that Chinese day,
the stone borders, universal ease,
the breeze-blocks of clouds over the century huts,
weeping cement and useless petrol.

Under the cherry- and apple-trees in our winter garden,
only barbed wire grows.

Инфернальные повторения

Бункера стены
Крупными буквами
Вы перестукивались
Рыжая сбрита щетина на пальцах
Иероглифика факелов и кинжалов
Словно в берлинском метро
Древне-готические стены
И сквозь решетку – струна антенны.

И здесь в аду
Не отвечали вы на допросах.
Крупно-горбатыми буквами
Вы перешептывались:
Время!
Нам не пристало, Иосиф,
Адольф!
Еще не настало, Иосиф.

Infernal Repetitions

You exchanged taps with each other,
taps and capital letters.
You knocked on the walls of the bunker.
Red bristle on your fingers was shaven off.
The whole place, with hieroglyphic
torches and daggers on the old Gothic walls,
resembled the Berlin underground.
The antenna string slipped through the bars.

In this strange kind of hell
you never answered questions
at the time of interrogations.
You exchanged gibbous capital letters,
you whispered to one another:
"We ought not to speak, Joseph."
"Our time hasn't come yet,
Adolf."

Сергей Бирюков
Sergey Biryukov

Sergey Biryukov was born in 1950 in Tambov. Having lived in Moscow, he is currently based in Halle, Germany. Having started writing poetry at the end of 1960s, he only saw his first poem published in a literary magazine in 1989. Since then, he has published many collections of his poems; the first of them, *The Muse of Zaum* (1980) and the most recent two, *The Run of Books* and *Calling* (both 2015). He also published the monograph entitled *Zevgma: Russian Poetry, Mannerism to Postmodernism* (1994), as well as a number of books on the history and theoretical aspects of Russian avant-garde. He was the founder and President of the Academy of Zaum, which includes Futurist poets from everywhere in Russia. His work has been translated into several European languages. He won first prize at the Berlin International Poetry Competition, and was the recipient of the Alexey Kruchenykh Poetry Award. He read from his poems at several international poetry festivals.

* * *

все меняется
прав гераклит
или кто там
неважно
все меня...
и по ком-то
звонит
колокольчик
бумажный

Everything Changes

everything changes
Heraclitus was right
or what was his name
never mind
everything changes me...
and a bell
tolls
for somebody
a paper bell

* * *

Тень
шорох тени
и нет хороших
в шорах
кто хорош?
рошхо рошхо!
Ни те, рох шо,
ни другие

Who's Good?

Shadows
rustling of shadows
and no good man
wears blinkers in the shade
who's good
goody-goofy-good?
Richard Roe, John Doe –
neither that shadow
nor the next

* * *

вы так же встаете
из кроватей
из могил
зверочеловеки
набираете еды
из животных
растений
и уносите
в могилу
Только надпись
настоящие растворены
в пространстве
или времени
над ними
нет плиты
нет

Beastmen

In the same old way
you get out of your beds
of your graves –
beastmen –
gather some food
rodents
vegetables
and take it all
back to your crypts

Inscriptions: signboards…
the genuine ones
dissolved in space
or in time
no tombstones
on their graves
none whatsoever

В скрипичном ключе

Рука подхвачена рукой
над нотой ля
октавы третьей.
Что слава сделала, другой
так не пометит.
То было время трудно-дней,
народного желанья славы.
Возможно ль выдумать людей
сложней, чем эти сплавы?
Терпением ожесточать –
какая стойкая привычка.
Разбей молчания печать,
скрипичный ключ, а не отмычка.

The Treble Clef

One hand is held up by another
over the note A
of a high octave.
What glory has achieved,
cannot be tamed.
Those were the days of the Chief
Difficulties and the all-out search for fame.
Can you possibly imagine
people as complex as metallic alloys?
Their black magic, their unchanging habit
of embittering a man by trying his patience.
What breaks the seal of silence
is the treble clef, not a picklock.

Новые сведения о Петрарке и Лауре

Лаура пишет письмо Петрарке
шрифтом Times New Roman
в интернет-тетрадке

письмо исчезает

Петрарка пишет сонет Лауре
пальцы бегут по клавиатуре

письмо исчезает

на платье Лауры осыпаются
букв лепестки

в этот миг
они так близки
что руку вот протяни
коснешься мизинца
левой руки

News of Petrarch and Laura

Laura types a letter to Petrarch
in the Times New Roman font
it's her blog

and it disappears

Petrarch types a sonnet for Laura
his fingers run along the keyboard

the sonnet disappears

the petals of syllables
fall onto Laura's frock

silence lingers
the two of them sit so close
he'd touch her little finger
should he stretch his right hand
into the Cyberland

Владимир Бурич
Vladimir Burich

Vladimir Burich (1932–1994) was born in Shakhty, Russia, and grew up in Kharkiv, Ukraine. In 1955, he graduated from Moscow State University, where he studied journalism. He later lived in Moscow working as an editor for the Molodaya Gvardiya Publishing House. His poetry was first published in 1961, but only achieved a certain degree of recognition in the 1980s and '90s when a few anthologies of Russian free verse poetry were published, *White Square* (1988), *Time X* (1989) and *The Anthology of Russian Vers Libre* (1991). Burich also wrote essays on free verse poetry in the times when it was relatively unknown in the USSR. He translated contemporary Polish, Czech and Serbian poetry into Russian. He died in Struga, Macedonia, during the Poetry Evenings festival, to which he was invited to read from his poems.

Я заглянул к себе ночью в окно

Я заглянул к себе ночью в окно
и увидел
что меня там нет

И понял
что меня может не быть

At Night I Looked into My Room Through the Window

At night I looked into my room through the window
and I noticed
that I wasn't there

And I realised
that my non-existence is entirely possible

* * *

Так и не смог доесть
золотую буханку дня

Посмотрел на часы
половина семидесятого

надо ложиться спать
гасить свет
в глазах

Руки можно поднять
чтобы капитулировать
чтобы взлететь

Half Past Seventies

I couldn't eat the whole
golden loaf of the day

I looked at my watch
half past seventies

time to go to bed
and switch off the light
in my eyes

hands can be raised
to give in

to fly up

* * *

Отцветут
опадут
лепестки галстуков
шелуха костюмов
кожура обуви
и останется
голый смысл моей жизни
на первый взгляд никому не нужной
как зеленые
несъедобные
семена картофеля

What Will Remain

They will cease to bloom
and drop down
the petals of neckties
the husk of costumes
shoe peels
what will remain
is the naked meaning of my life
no one will seem to need it
just like green
inedible
potato seeds

Германия-1984

Я захотел заглянуть в пасть зверю

а увидел
маленькие домики под красной черепицей
высунувшихся из окон старушек
детей идущих в кирху на концерт Баха
желтые кусты форзиций бледно-розовые соцветия очиток
кружку пива стоящую на тротуаре
рядом с мастером укладывающим плиты

Он подмигнул мне
и весело крикнул:
– Рус сдавайся!

Germany, 1984

I wanted to look inside the beast's mouth

but what I saw were
little houses with red tile roofs
old women leaning out of the windows
children going to the church for a concert of Bach's music
yellow furze bushes, pale pink inflorescences
a beer mug on the pathway
next to a worker laying tiles

He winked at me
and shouted cheerfully:
"Rus, surrender!"

* * *

На бульваре
закрыв лицо от страха газетой
сидят
в ожидании смерти
пенсионеры

Старый Христос с Иудой играют в шашки
Разбойники хвастаются тем что их тоже распинали
Мария вяжет варежки внукам

У ног ее
дети
из песка
строят
Вавилонскую башню

On the Boulevard

On the boulevard
old age pensioners sit
covering their faces with newspapers
in fear
in anticipation of death

Aged Christ plays checkers with Judas
robbers brag about having been crucified too
Saint Mary knits mittens for her granddaughters

At her feet
children
make
the Tower of Babel
out of sand

Владимир Эрль
Vladimir Earle

Vladimir Earle (pen name of Vladimir Gorbunov) was born in St. Petersburg in 1947. Having worked as a fireman, a laboratory assistant and a watchman, he now works as a librarian. He started writing poetry in 1962 as a fifteen-year-old. In a few years' time he became a member of the so-called Helenooct group of young poets that existed between 1966 and 1971. His poems were widely published in Samizdat and in the Western Russian-language magazines. Since the years of perestroika he has published three critically acclaimed collections of his rather experimental poetry, *Helenooctism* (1993), *The Grass, the Grass* (1995), *The Book of King* (2009), *Yesterday and The Day After Tomorrow* (2012), a book of non-fiction, *In Search of the Lost Xeif* (1999), as well as many essays on the Russian literature of the twentieth century. A volume of his *Collected Poems* appeared in Saint-Petersburg in 2015. Among the authors he has translated into Russian are Samuel Beckett and Franz Kafka. He was awarded the Andrey Belyi Prize for Poetry (1986) and the David Burliuk Prize for life-long commitment to experimental poetry (1991).

* * *

Я в осень вошел, как во взгляд,
как в тихий туман реки.
Зеленые тростники
качались зачем-то вдали…
Я в осень вошел, как в реку,
охваченную тишью снов.
И легионы слов
качались где-то вдали.
Я в осень вошел, как в слова,
потерянные кем-то вдали.

Autumn

I entered into autumn as into a glance,
or into a quiet mist on the river's face.
Green canes
were swaying in the distance.
I entered into autumn as into the river
embraced by the silence of dreams.
Myriads of words
were swaying in the distance.
I entered into autumn as into the words
somebody had lost in the distance.

* * *

Преграда сна –
как ветер, рвущий в клочья
деревья гибкие.
Вчера – я снова жил.
Сегодня – только сплю;
проходит вереница
пустых мечтаний.
Волны ль это –
или песок – сыпучий, легкий и бесцветный?
Как будто дождь…

The Barrier of Sleep

The barrier of sleep –
is like the wind that rips these supple trees
to pieces.
Yesterday I lived again.
Today I'm only sleeping.
A row of empty dreams
passes before my eyes.
Are these the waves? Or maybe
sand, free-flowing, colourless and light?
It resembles rain…

* * *

Когда люди имеют мнения,
они обмениваются ими.
Когда люди не имеют мнений,
они обмениваются отсутствием мнений.

Opinions

When people have opinions,
they swap them.
When people have no opinions,
they swap the absence of opinions.

Эвридика

Пламя свечи виновато марьяжит.
Меняется форма, рождается шорох –
Орфея плач. Он слышит
удар руки по струнам звонкой лиры…
Связует нить воззрения паука,
повисшего над миром
мельчайших тканей, –
тянется за словом моим паутина –
златого дня немыслимый конец.

И пьет Орфей настой из терпких слов,
забывшись сном, над лирою склоняясь
и наблюдая гладь
сиреневого Стикса.

Eurydice

A candle flickers guiltily.
The flame changes its shape, and causes a rustle,
which is the weeping of Orpheus. He hears
his hand strike the strings of the resonant lyre…
The thread of spider's thoughts
the one that hangs above the world
of fine-grained substance
cobweb trails my words,
such an unthinkable end of the golden day.

And so Orpheus drinks an extract of bitter words,
which leaves him sunk into a reverie,
bent over the lyre and the glassy surface
of the lilac Styx.

* * *

О!
О, чешуя на руках!
ребра мои окружает вода
плещет плавник за спиной
воздух сгущается.

О!
О, тени в подводных садах –
иногда
вырастают стеной
позади.

Under Water

Ah!
O these scales on my hands!
my ribs are surrounded by water
the fin behind my back makes splashes
the air thickens.

Ah!
O these shadows in the underwater gardens –
sometimes they
build themselves up like a wall
behind you.

Михаил Файнерман
Mikhail Finerman

Mikhail Finerman (1946–2003) was born in Moscow. Having graduated from Moscow State University of Printing Arts, he worked as an engineer, a tour-guide and a translator. In the early 1980s he joined the poetic movement called Personae. He described himself as a Zen Buddhist. Most of his poems were gathered together and published posthumously in his only collection, *The Finch in Flight* (Moscow, 1995), to critical acclaim. He also translated Slovakian poetry into Russian, and published an essay on Russian free verse.

* * *

Касаясь
языком то нёба, то дёсен,
они не кровоточат, но болят,
дымлю, касаюсь,
касаюсь снова и снова,
думаю о своём.

Touching

Touching my palate,
then my gum
with my tongue;
no bleeding, but they hurt.
I smoke, and touch again,
time and again.
I think about my innermost.

* * *

Как жёсткая зелень
арабских лугов
пробивается
сквозь любовь и ненависть
к высотам еврейского неба,
так и я
тоскую:
я ничего не помню
и ничего не хочу.

Yearning

Like robust green shoots
of Arabian meadows
that break through
love and hate
to the heights of the Jewish sky,
I have a sense
of yearning:
I remember nothing,
and want nothing.

* * *

Свет предосенний редок,
как колпак у чахоточного больного
в начале нашего века,
веки смежая, пытаешься
дотянуться
до полочки на потолке, тени и тени, немые –
имя
все равно твое.

Name

The light of pre-autumn is scarce
as the cap of a consumptive patient
from the beginning of the century.
Blinking, you try to reach
the shelf under the ceiling;
shadows follow shadows, dumb ones –
your name
is still yours.

※ ※ ※

Звери не хоронят своих мертвецов,
и зима им не ведома.
А мы дрожим, мерзнем,
жмемся друг к другу.
– Ну что там теперь?
расскажи.

Winter

Beasts don't bury their dead,
and have no knowledge of winter.
But we tremble, we freeze,
we squeeze closer together.
"Well, what's happening there these days?
Tell us."

* * *

очутиться одному, на ветру,
одному,
на ветру...

To Find Yourself

To find yourself alone in the wind;
alone,
in the wind…

Руслан Галимов
Ruslan Galimov

Ruslan Galimov (1946–1982) was a Tatar poet born in Chistopol and educated in Moscow. During his life-time, only a few of his poems appeared in Russian literary magazines and anthologies. He died of leukaemia in 1982. Three collections of his poems and short stories have been published posthumously and garnered critical acclaim. He is regarded as a prominent writer of Russian-language free-verse poetry.

Прогноз

Сегодня в Душанбе
дождь,
а может, женщина
вдруг вспомнила меня.
Ее огромные глаза
застыли на дороге,
по которой я не приду
никогда

Forecast

It is raining today
in Dushanbe,
or maybe a woman
suddenly remembered me.
Her huge eyes are
glued to the road
that will never bring me
back to her.

* * *

Я долго был уверен,
что у меня прямые ноги
и широкие плечи.

Но однажды
маленькая женщина
рассмеялась мне в лицо,
сказав, что я кривоногий
и хожу, сутулясь.

Я с удивлением заметил,
что в общем-то она права.
И с тех пор никогда не хожу
перед нею раздетым.

In General, She Was Right

For a long time I thought
I had straight legs
and broad shoulders.

One day
a little woman
laughed in my face,
saying that I was bow-legged
and walked with a stoop.

I was surprised to notice
that, in general, she was right.
From then on I never appear
in front of her undressed.

* * *

Прекрасно общаясь
со своими соотечественниками
на одном из прекраснейших языков мира,
мы до сих пор еще
пытаемся договориться,
не понимая друг друга…

Agreeability

Smoothly communicating
with our compatriots
in one of the most beautiful languages of the world,
we're still trying to come
to an agreement
without understanding each other...

* * *

Я думал – это ГРОМ!
А это проехала мусорка,
гремя железными баками.

Я думал – это друг.
Открываю дверь, пришли
За долгами.

Я думал... думал...
О чем бы еще подумать?..

Включаю репродуктор:
«Советский Союз обогнал Америку
по производству яиц на душу населения».

Пойду куплю
может подешевели.

What Can Man Think About?

Thought 'twas THUNDER
but it was a garbage lorry
clanking its metallic scoops.

Thought 'twas a friend calling on me
but at the threshold there were
debt collectors.

I thought and thought again…
What can man think about?

I turned on the radio…
"Soviet Union has overtaken America
in egg production per head."

Shall I go buy them, eggs?
Maybe the price has gone down…

* * *

Сегодня думал я о смерти,
бродил по лужам,
щурился на солнце.
Сегодня встретил я
двадцать девять
беременных женщин
и решил,
что не страшно умереть.

Today

Today I've been pondering
death.
I walked across puddles;
sunlight made me squint.
Today I met
twenty-nine pregnant women,
and decided that dying
is not such a scary thing.

Татьяна Трауз
Tatyana Grauz

Tatyana Grauz (pen name of Tatyana Griolooz) was born in Chelyabinsk in 1964. She was educated at the Moscow Medical Academy and at the Russian Academy of Theatre Arts, and worked in Moscow as a theatre director, occasionally appearing on stage and in feature films as an actress. She has published three collections of her textual and visual poems, *Too Much Space* (2004), *More Transparent than the Sky* (2005) and *Forest-Lake-Garden* (2014). Her poems have been translated into English, Swedish, Japanese and Chuvash. She won the David Burliuk Prize for life-long commitment to experimental poetry.

Утренний сон

ночью в разрушенном доме
кто-то стучался в закрытую дверь
кто-то входил в опустевшие комнаты
жёлтые листья – капли увядшего света
по подоконнику шелестели тревожно

Morning Dream

at night someone was knocking
at the closed door of a ruined house
someone entered the empty rooms
yellow leaves—drops of withered light—
rustled uneasily on the windowsill

* * *

в свете июля зелень паслёна
    х р у с т а л ь н а
нужно ль ещё что-нибудь?
может быть отсвет дрожащий
    зелёный
в воде голубой?

July's Light

in July's light the emerald of the nightshade
        crystal clear
do we need anything else?
maybe a shimmering sheen of
        green
in the blue of the water?

* * *

неба-житель-бабочка
вздохом крыльев встревожила
л е т а б л а ж е н с т в о

Butterfly

a resident of the sky
butterfly
flapped her wings
disturbed *s u m m e r b l i s s*

Неяркое солнце

в одноразовом дне неделимо
сияние сада
холодок синевы
и боярышника багровые пятна
и неяркое солнце
и дождь переменный

такая казалось бы монотонная жизнь
такие скупые подробности
будто перед разлукой
разглядывает припоминая душа

Soft Sun

Inside a disposable day they are indivisible:
        the shining of the garden
     the chilly blueness
the crimson stains of the hawthorn
        the soft sun
   and the fickle rain

such a seemingly monotonous life
  so few details
      as though the soul before departure
scrutinises them trying to remember

Апрель-голубка

проточный свет
        день чистопрудный
апрель-голубка в теплынь недремлющего неба
    на льдинке солнца незаметно проплывает
как мы быть может
        может быть когда-то

April-Dove

flowing light
              the clear-pond day
April-Dove in the warmth of the watchful sky
      floating by insensibly on a little
              ice flow of the Sun
as we will perhaps
            perhaps one day

Дмитрий Григорьев
Dmitry Grigoriev

Dmitry Grigoriev was born in 1960 in St. Petersburg, where he still lives. A graduate of Leningrad State University, he travelled the world extensively, and wrote poetry, however he wasn't allowed to publish anything until perestroika. Some of his poems, though, found their way onto the pages of a few American Russian-language magazines. At the beginning of 1990s three collections of his poems appeared in St. Petersburg. He is now regarded as one of the most important St. Petersburg poets of his generation. A volume of his *Selected Unpublished Poems* came out in 1992. Since then, he has published three novels, a book of his short stories, a travel book and seven collections of poetry, including *Crossroads* (1995), *Fiery Yard-Keeper* (2005), *The Other Photographer* (2009) and *New Fairy Tales* (2011).

* * *

Во тьме ты светишься…
Ночные мотыльки
стучатся в твою кожу,
на крыльях каждого –
мои глаза…
А я перебираю буквы,
похожие на яблочные зерна,
и слова не могу сказать…

Night

In the darkness, your shining…
Night moths
tap on your skin;
each wing
shows my eyes.
I leaf through letters
that resemble apple seeds,
but no words find a way out…

* * *

Положи мои слова на землю,
утрамбуй их ногами, чтобы не поднимались,
чтобы сеточка подошвы отпечаталась на каждом,
чтобы никто их не трогал и,
проходя мимо, каждый говорил: «Бросовая вещь».
Чтобы их засыпало снегом,
чтобы на них мочились собаки,
чтобы они были незаметны словно
прошлогодние листья,
чтобы, глядя на них,
говорили: «Земля…»

Тогда подними мои слова к небу.

Words

Lay my words on the ground,
tread them down, ram them firmly,
so that the pattern of the sole leaves a mark on them,
and no one ever touches them,
and each passer-by mutters: "Such a useless thing" –
and snow covers them,
dogs urinate on them,
and they become indistinguishable
like rotten leaves,
and people, looking at them, say:
"That's clay."

Then raise them up to the sky.

* * *

Ночью:
серые мотыльки прячутся
в складках моей одежды.
Они наполняют мой костюм,
шелест их крыльев похож
на мой шепот.
А когда на улице
зажигают фонари,
они вместе летят на свет,
и костюм движется,
словно это я иду, скрывая лицо
под глубоко надвинутой шапкой,
но мои глаза – лишь рисунок на крыльях,
и душа моя – пыль.

Shades of Night

At night
grey moths hide themselves
in secret folds of my clothes.
They fill my suit.
Rustling of their wings sounds like
my whisper.

When all the street lamps
begin to shine
the moths fly up to them –
and my suit seems to be moving
as though I walk hiding my face,
my hat pulled over my eyes.

Ah, my eyes are circles on butterflies' wings,
and my soul is dust.

* * *

Мне говорили:
Полезные вещи нельзя на помойку,
полезные вещи еще пригодятся.
Мне подарили большую коробку:
в эту коробку поместится много
полезных вещей.
Мне нравится эта коробка,
она стоит улыбаясь,
в ней очень тепло и уютно
и я в ней легко умещаюсь,
а значит, я очень полезен
и, значит, еще пригожусь.

Not Rubbish

They used to say,
Don't scrap good things,
they will come in handy.
They presented me with a cardboard box
big enough to store
loads of good things in it…

I have a liking for this box
that stands here smiling.
It is big enough to accommodate me.
I feel cosy in it, I am warm.

Maybe this means that I am a good thing
and will come in handy.

***

Рыбаки возвращаются без улова,
говорят:
– Река разлилась и вода замутилась.

Рыбаки возвращаются,
рассыпаясь каплями, словно дождь,
говорят:
– По реке идёт грязь, давно идёт грязь,
и рыбы уже не найдешь.

Но лишь высохнет наша одежда,
мы снова пойдем к реке.

Fishermen

Fishermen come back empty-handed.
Fishermen say,
The water is high, the water is troubled.

Fishermen come back –
and spill and scatter like rain-drops.
Fishermen say,
Mud has long been floating down the river,
and now the fish are gone.

But we shall return to the river
as soon as our clothes dry.

Елена Кацюба
Elena Katsuba

Elena Katsuba was born in 1946 in Kamensk near Rostov, and educated at Kazan State University. She has lived in Moscow for many years working as a journalist. Her first poem was published in 1963. Since then her poems and short stories have appeared only in unofficial periodicals in Russia (samizdat) and abroad. Since 1999, she has published three collections of poems, including *eR-eL* (2002), *Igr Rai* (2003), *The Testimony of the Moon* (2008) and *Those Who Stare at the Flame* (2014), as well as a dictionary of palindromes. She is the founding member of the DOOS group of poets (with Konstantin Kedrov).

Свеча

Свеча боится темноты

Чем больше страх свечи – тем ярче свет

Чем ярче свет – тем жизнь свечи короче

Чем жизнь короче – тем сильнее страх

Чем страх сильней – тем ярче свет свечи

Чем ярче свет – тем жизнь короче

Чем жизнь короче – тем сильнее страх...

Candle

The candle is afraid of darkness

The stronger the candle's fear the brighter the light

The brighter the light the shorter the candle's life

The shorter the life the stronger the fear

The stronger the fear the brighter the candle's light

The brighter the light the shorter the life

The shorter the life the stronger the fear...

* * *

Дождь смотрит на бабочку сквозь стекло
Бабочка смотрит сквозь дождь
Дождь никогда не забудет бабочку
Бабочка уже забыла дождь

Butterfly and the Rain

The rain looks at a butterfly through the glass
The butterfly looks through the rain
The rain will never forget the butterfly
The butterfly has already forgotten the rain

Вариант

…Тогда сотворил Бог зеркало и отразился в нем.
Так Адам создан был, и Бог его любил как самого себя.
Дал Бог Адаму зеркало, посмотрелся Адам в зеркало –
так Ева явилась.
И любил ее Адам, как самого себя.
Посмотрелись Адам и Ева друг в друга, как в зеркало,
и появились у них дети,
и Ева любила их больше самой себя,
оттого дети любили только себя,
и убил Авель Каина.
В гневе разбил Бог зеркало и развеял по свету.
Оттого мы видим мир не как создал Бог,
но как отражает зеркальный прах.

An Apocryphal Story

…And God made a mirror, and the mirror reflected Him.
So Adam was created, and God liked Adam as much
as he liked himself. God gave Adam the mirror. Adam
looked at himself – and Eve came into the world,
and Adam liked her as much as he liked himself.
Adam and Eve saw each other just as they saw themselves
in the mirror – and unto them children were born,
and Eve loved them more than she loved herself.
And the children loved nobody but themselves – and Abel
rose against Cain his brother and slew him.
God was enraged; he broke the mirror and scattered
its splinters. And now we see the world not as it was made
but as reflected in the grains of mirror sand…

На свалке заменимых нет!

Любой стандартный предмет
на свалке приобретает индивидуальность.

Все новые башмаки новы одинаково –
каждый рваный башмак рван по-своему!

There's Nothing Replaceable in the Dump!

Any standard item in the dump
gets an individuality.

All new shoes are equally new –
but every ragged one is torn in its own way!

* * *

Жизнь сложена из лепестков розы
внутри которой развернут сад
где растет всего одна роза
размером с целый сад

ключ потерян

The Rose Garden

Life is formed of rose petals
there is a garden within that rose
and there's a single rose in it
as big as the whole garden

the key to the gate is lost

Константин Кедров
Konstantin Kedrov

Konstantin Kedrov was born in 1942 in Moscow, and educated at Moscow University. Poet, essayist and philosopher, he started writing poetry at the end of the 1950s. In 1984 he founded the DOOS group of poets (with Elena Katsuba). He is editor of the Moscow-based *Zhurnal Poetov / The PO Journal*. Since the beginning of perestroika he has published many collections of his poems, including *Computer of Love* (1990), *Vroutselet* (1993), *The Gamut of Hamlet's Bodies* (1994), *Ulysses and Navsikaya* (1997), *Sam ist Dat* (2003) and *The Conductor of Silence* (2009). A volume of his collected poems entitled *Or* appeared in Moscow in 2002. He has also published three books of his essays on literature and philosophy, including *Poetic Cosmos* (1989). In 2003, he was the recipient of the GRAMMY.ru Poet of the Year Award.

Иероглиф Бога

возможно
что Бог
в середине Китая
летает витая
витает летая

Hieroglyph for God

perhaps
God can be found
in middle China
wind hovering
hover flying

Аэроэра

Все что пережито – не пережито
Мы предопределены
но не предрешены
Эра аэродромов
уходит в прошлое
Наступает эра
аэро-
тишины

Aero Era

All we've experienced
we haven't really experienced
Our destiny is prearranged
but not predetermined
The era of airports
is becoming a thing of the past
what follows is an era
of aero-
silence

Лодка

К Востоку уплывает безвесельная птица
Она на мертвых крыльях пылает в глубине
Безликой базиликой Озирис озарился
Осиротел Озирис в безносой вышине
Заманчив этот облик
и этот запах пряный
из девственного лона
в межзвездное руно
Озирис пьяный
Дионис пьяный
уткнулся в дно

Keel

An oarless bird swims to the East
She is ablaze in the depth, on dead wings
Osiris shines like a faceless basilica
He has become orphaned in the noseless heights
He looks desirable
and the smell of spice is wafted
from the womb of a virgin
to the interstellar fleece
Osiris is drunk
Dionysus drunk too
he has buried his head at the bottom

Свирель

За мной крадется вор с тупой свирелью
в ней все заполнено очами
слепой свирелью стал туманный посох
врастающий в туман
гремит туманом
свирельная ночная мгла
зрачки перебирая
окутанный свирелью горизонт
встает из праха
мертвый как младенец
спеленатый свирелью грозовой
слепые роды
грозовой свирели

Reed Pipe

A blunt pipe-wielding thief is shadowing me
with a pipe thick with eyes
a misty staff has turned into a blind pipe
growing into the fog
the fog is thundering
the night haze piping
counting the pupils
a piped horizon
rises from the ashes
dead as a baby
swaddled with a thundering pipe
it gives a blind birth
to a thundering pipe

Крылья

Эти крылья –
справа – слева –
спереди – сзади –
это только одно крыло
преломленное
во всех пространствах
где нечетнокрылые
улетают
крыльями внутрь
здесь тайна твоя и моя
с нечетным количеством крыльев
В четырех измерениях души
сплетают
раковые уши.

Wings

These wings –
on the right – on the left –
at the front – behind –
they are just one wing
refracted
in all dimensions
where those with an odd number of wings
fly away
turning their wings inward.
This is a secret, yours and mine,
a secret with an odd number of wings.
In some four-dimensional space
souls tat
acoustic crayfish lace.

Игорь Холин
Igor Kholin

Igor Kholin (1920–1999) was born and lived in Moscow. In his youth, he was employed as a waiter, then joined the Russian Army, fought in World War II, was wounded, and retired when the war ended. At the beginning of the 1950s he became a member of the now famous Lianozovo group of poets and painters. Under the Communists, his poems appeared only in émigré magazines, such as *Strelets/The Archer* and *Tretya Volna/Third Wave*. In 1989, his first poetry book entitled *Poems with Dedications* was published in Paris in Russian and subsequently reprinted in Moscow. His next collection appeared in 1995. At the end of the 1990s, he published a number of his short stories. After his death in 1999, an ample volume of his *Collected Poems* appeared in Moscow, followed by another big volume, this time of his *Collected Stories*.

* * *

Камера
Инженера Крамера
В ней
Идет обработка людей
В смысле
Единства идей
Тук
Тук
Тук
Работает ультразвук
У Нилина
Лишняя извилина
Жилину
Добавить извилину

Cramer's Camera

Engineer Cramer
Invented a camera
Inside it
They are processing people
To achieve
Unification of ideas
Rat-tat
Rat-tat
Rat-tat
Ultrasound in action
Nilin has
An extra gyrus
Zhilin
To be added an extra gyrus

* * *

Э. Иодковскому

Если ты одинок,
Если тебе не с кем поговорить
Зайди
К самому себе
Поговори
Сам с собой

Poem for Edmund Iodkovsky

If you are lonely
If you have no one to talk to –
Why not
Visit
And try to talk
To yourself?

Из военного цикла

Командир батареи
Безусый
Парнишка
Рассматривал в бинокль
Поле
Утыканное
Ромашками
И васильками
Затем
Вдохнул
Полной грудью
Окопную вонь
Крикнул
Огооонь
И все полетело
Вверх тормашками

From "The War River"

The gun-commander
A young lad
Wearing no moustache
Used his field glass
To examine the field

All about were dotted
Daisies and cornflowers

The lad breathed in
The trench stink
And screamed:
Fire!

Topsy-turvyness
The world is in a mess

* * *

Ни звезды
Ни креста
Ни черта
Волосы
Вместо травы
Торчат
Из земли
На братской могиле

Common Grave

No stars
No crosses
No nothing

Instead of grass
Hair
Sticks
Out of the ground
At the common grave

* * *

Одни говорят
Что я гений
Я говорю
Это
Действительно так
Другие говорят
Бездарен
Я подтверждаю
Третьи говорят
Я убил человека
Киваю головой
Все что говорят люди
Правда
Сотканная
Из пустоты

Truths

Some say
I am a man of genius
I never
Deny it
Others assert that
I am dull
I readily
Agree
Somebody alleges that
I murdered a man
I nod
Everything people say
Is a truth
Woven from
Emptiness

Виктор Кривулин
Viktor Krivulin

Viktor Krivulin (1944–2001) was born in Krasnodon, Ukraine. From 1947 he lived in St. Petersburg. He was educated at Leningrad State University, where he studied Russian and Italian literature. In the 1970s, he was closely associated with two of the Russian samizdat magazines, *37* and *Severnaya Pochta/Northern Post*, where he published his poems and essays. He belonged to the so-called New Leningrad school of poetry, which also included Joseph Brodsky, Elena Shvarts and Sergey Stratanovsky. After perestroika, he became involved in politics, and was at the head of the St. Petersburg branch of Democratic Russia, the pro-democracy political party. Among his critically acclaimed collections are *A Concert of Requests* (1993), *Borderland* (1994), *Bathing in Jordan* (1998), and *Poems of the Jubilee Year* (2001). His poems have been translated into many European languages. In 1978, he was awarded the first ever Andrey Belyi Prize for Poetry.

Рысь

золотоглазую мы не заметили Рысь
когда она следит не щурясь, не мигая
за солнцем, нет, за митингом:
сошлись
они стоят как тишина большая
защитники всего что ползает плывет
что ходит посуху и над землей летает...
но поздно уже... вечер... холодает
и, постояв, расходится народ

Lynx

that golden-eyed Lynx, we didn't notice it
as it watched the Sun,
oh no, it watched the meeting,
not even blinking…
they gather and stand still like greater silence,
those protectors of everything that crawls, or swims,
or walks on dry land, or flies over…
but it is getting late… and growing cold…
and soon the people drift apart

Пока мы изобретали рай

когда мы конструировали Запад
на сорока внутрисоветских языках
как некий Рай в золовых рукавах
как Ханаан, какой не занят
никем – и только нам обетован, –
мы видели египетские казни
вокруг себя, но жили безопасней
Обломова: схожденье на диван
святого духа с эмигрантским чтивом
портрет Набокова с пурпурною каймой…
когда ходил Господь по нищенским квартирам
и призывал на родину, домой –
в Европу, в Индию ли, в Палестину,
где Пуп Земли, а мы всегда не там…

While We Invented Paradise

while we constructed the West
in the forty Soviet languages,
just like some sort of paradise in our ashen hands,
or like Canaan, unoccupied and promised
to ourselves – we saw the punishment of Egypt
but lived much safer than Oblomov*:
we would come down, the way the Holy Spirit did,
to a sofa, holding an émigré journal
and facing a portrait of Nabokov in the purple frame…

meanwhile, the Lord called on our beggarly abodes
and summoned us to our real homelands,
to Europe, or to India, sometimes to Palestine,
the hub of the Universe
where we are always missing…

---

* A personage, an idler, in the novel of the same name by Ivan Goncharov.

Книги и люди

худо, конечно, с какого конца ни возьми
но может быть, из-за того
полуослепшие книги тоже казались людьми
и скрывали преступное с ними родство

прятали а если за стенкой затихал сосед –
бережно – как шуршит папиросный слой! –
обнажали какой-нибудь порфироносный портрет
полоску с гольбеиновой Пьетой

Books and Men

indeed, it was bad from any point of view
but maybe because of that
weak-sighted books acquired a strange resemblance
to people and so had to conceal forbidden kinship

however, when a neighbour calmed down behind the wall
they would uncover cautiously—
the flimsy paper rustling timidly—
some regal portrait – or Holbein's Pietà

Над гранитной фабрикой

над гранитной фабричкой агатовая пыль
крошка ониксовая опаловая труха

тут тебе и творчество и лаборатория стиха
и традиции и национальный стиль
полудрагоценный камень превращается в утиль
в пепельницу или в тельце петуха

и полуслепой приемщицы ОТК
слабый штемпель
не смываемый
на века

Over the Granite Factory

in the air over the small granite factory, there are
hyalite crumbs, tiny bits of onyx and agathic dust

a classic example of a creative workshop
and poetic laboratory, a real booster of traditions
and the national style… semiprecious stone turns
into rubbish, like a figurine of a rooster or an ash-tray –

and a quality inspector, the weak-sighted female,
stamps each object in the same way
with a pale mark,
never to be erased

Финал

Резные двери в деревянных розах.
Двойное растворение вовнутрь –
и в утренний сужающийся воздух
мы втянуты, как завитки волны, –
как вихри света, обтекающие утварь,
в один источник сведены,
в единый узел.

The End

Carved doors with wooden roses.
A double dissolution inwards –
and we get drawn into the converging morning air
like curls of a wave, like vortexes of light
that flow around pots and pans
summarised into one source,
into a single node.

Анатолий Кудрявицкий
Anatoly Kudryavitsky

Anatoly Kudryavitsky was born in 1954 in Moscow to a Polish father and half-Irish mother. Having lived in Russia and Germany, he has been based in Dublin since the beginning of the century. Educated at Moscow Medical University, he later worked as a researcher in immunology, a journalist and a literary translator. Since 1989 he has published three novels, a book of short stories, seven collections of his Russian poems, the most recent being *The Book of Gimmicks: Collected Prose Poems* (Evgeny Stepanov Publishing, 2017), as well as a collection of his English poems entitled *Shadow of Time* (Goldsmith Press, 2005) and three collections of his English-language haiku. His new collection of prose poems in English titled *The Two-Headed Man and the Paper Life* is forthcoming in the USA from Plume Editions / MadHat Press in 2018. An anthology of contemporary German-language poetry in his translations to English entitled *Coloured Handprints* has been published by Dedalus Press in 2015; an anthology of contemporary Ukrainian poetry in his translation to English entitled *The Frontier* has been published by Glagoslav Publications in 2017. He won the David Burliuk Prize for life-long commitment to experimental poetry (2010).

Камерная музыка

Зрелость входит с корзинкой
золотистых слив
говорит: не ешь

внутри моей комнаты –
другая
незримая

день стряхивает цвета
сливы тоже становятся
незримыми

а я теперь похож
на старое сливовое дерево
я дышу – и листья шелестят

Chamber Music

Maturity comes with a punnet
of golden plums.
It says, refrain from eating the fruit.

Inside my room
there's another,
an invisible one.

As the day sheds its colours,
the plums too become
indiscernible.

And I am beginning to resemble
an old plum tree;
its leaves rustle as I breathe.

Бунин. Портрет с отсутствием объекта

В зеркале за его спиной плывет
вчерашний день
красные флаги и казачьи штандарты
его отражение –
полый силуэт

Кого-то втискивают
в оставленное им пространство
втискиваемый не помещается
кряхтит
потом устраивается как-то –

и трещит каркас
параллелей и меридианов

Bunin: Portrait with the Person Missing

In the mirror behind his back
recent times are floating
red flags and standards of the Cossacks
his reflection
a hollow silhouette

into the space he left
a man is being squeezed
he can't go in
groans
then somehow manages –

and the framework of parallels and meridians
cracks all over the globe

Иуда

Он прихлебывает небесное желе
в бороде стрекочут кузнечики
в животе разбухает уродливая планетка

он развертывает свиток где сказано
«Камешки что ты родишь
вырастут в горы»

звуки свистулек брызжут на осины
серебром
он сломанное ребро мира
он жив он есть

Judas

He slurps the blue sky jelly.
Crickets chirr in his beard;
a little ugly planet swells inside him.

He unrolls the scroll that reads:
"If you give birth to pebbles,
they will grow into mountains."

Tin whistle music sprinkles yew trees
with silver. He's the world's broken rib.
He's alive.
He is.

Незримое кино

На экране моей телефонной книжки
зеленое кино:
рушатся дома
умирают
уходят в изгнание
люди

для постороннего глаза –
имена
цифры

The Invisible Cinema

On the screen of my
address book
a green movie:
houses collapsing
people going into exile
dying

To an outsider's eye
some names
digits

Гибель МН-17

Гигантский подсолнух гибнет в небесах.
Отправь дождь обратно в облака,
выключи язычки пламени
голубой васильковой горелки.

Чернозем всегда говорит с собою;
радио тоже.
Проснись. Взгляни, как тают звезды.
Утони снова во сне.

The Shooting Down of MH17

A huge sunflower dying in the sky…
Send the rain back to the clouds,
switch off the tiny stove-fire flames
of the bluets.

Black soil always talks to itself,
and so does the radio.
Wake up, watch the stars thaw.
Sink back into sleep.

Александр Макаров-Кротков
Alexander Makarov-Krotkov

Alexander Makarov-Krotkov (pen name of Alexander Makarov) was born in 1959 in Tyumen. He now lives in Moscow, and works as a journalist. He started writing poetry in the 1980s, and his first poem appeared in a literary magazine in 1989. Since then, he has published three collections of his poetry miniatures including *Deserter* (1995), *Nevertheless* (2002), *Concrete Sonnet* (2004), *And Then Everywhere* (2007). He read from his poems at literary festivals in Germany and Italy. His work has been translated into several European languages, and he was awarded the Grand Prix at the International Poetry Festival in Salerno, Italy (1992).

* * *

> К.

хорошо выпить водки
в любую погоду
хорошо знать что время
кончается вместе со смертью
у меня еще есть в запасе завтра
которое пересекаешь ты

For K.

vodka is a treat
whatever the weather
it is nice to know that time
comes to an end when we die
I still have tomorrow
that you will cross over

* * *

Внезапно сбежало лето.

Янис Рицос

холодно-свинцовая масса
напоминает море

на набережной
два-три человека
в предвкушении солнца –
ощущении чуда

и я
вопросительным знаком
на шершавой скамейке
назойливо жду ответа

On the Quays

Summer suddenly fled.

—Iannis Ritsos

this cold leaden mass of water
resembles the sea

on the quays
two or three men
wait for the sun
for a miracle yet to happen

I too sit there on a flaking bench
an interrogation mark
waiting for some answer
determinedly

* * *

тихо так воет собачка
словно хочет повеситься
а не умеет

The Doggy

a doggy is whining – oh, how quietly!
as if it wants to hang itself
but doesn't know how

Стокгольм

> Хансу Бьёркегрену

вот город
вот голос
речь иноземная
как морская болезнь

город на островах
причал катер качка

от острова к острову
от человека к человеку
и сладок уже звук
недоступной речи

засыпаю
без снотворного

Stockholm

(for Hans Bjorkegren)

here's the city
here's the voice
foreign speech
like sea sickness

city on the islands
a pier a boat a pitching

from island to island
from man to man
and incomprehensible speech
already sounds sweet

I fall asleep
without sleeping pills

Джеймс Джойс глазами советского читателя

читаешь в книге:
дублин
туман
катафалк
кладбище
отзывается сердце:
москва
кремль
мавзолей
владимир
ильич

A Soviet Reader's Remark on James Joyce

you read in his book:
Dublin
fog
a hearse
a graveyard
your heart echoes:
Moscow
the Kremlin
the Mausoleum
Vladimir Ilyich

Арво Метс
Arvo Mets

Arvo Mets (1937–1997) was born in Estonia, and educated at St. Petersburg University and at the Literary Institute in Moscow. He lived most of his life in Moscow, where he edited several literary magazines, including *Novy Mir / New World*. He started writing poetry in the early 1960s, and also translated Estonian poetry into Russian. Three critically acclaimed collections of his poetry miniatures were published in Moscow and Tallinn. His *Selected Poems* appeared in Moscow in 1992. His poems have since been translated into eight European languages.

* * *

Поэт стоит в очереди за вермишелью.
Здесь же и его почитательницы.
Поэту немного стыдно.
Он стоял на эстраде,
словно маленький принц,
который никогда не ест.

The Poet

The poet stands in a queue for spaghetti.
His female admirers there too.
The poet is slightly ashamed:
he appeared on stage
like a little prince
that didn't seem to need nourishment.

* * *

Исчезаю в весне,
в толпе,
в лужах,
в синеве.
И не ищите.
Мне так хорошо…

Absentee

I fade into spring
or into a crowd
or into a puddle
sometimes into the blue
there's no sense in looking for me:
I feel fine

* * *

Молодые девушки
похожи лицом
на небо,
на ветер,
на облака.
Потом из них получаются
верные жены,
лица которых похожи
на дома,
на мебель,
на хозяйственные сумки.
Но их дочери
вновь похожи лицом
на небо, ветер
и весенние ручейки.

Resemblance

Young girls
resemble in looks
the sky,
the wind,
the clouds above.

Later they make
devoted wives
whose faces remind us
of houses,
furniture,
carrier bags.

Still, their daughters
resemble in looks
the sky, the wind
and streamlets in springtime.

* * *

Безденежный человек
ходит по городу.
Туманные звезды
дрожат на морозе.

Безденежный человек –
безрукий человек,
безногий человек,
безглазый человек.

В городе зажигаются огни,
и все видят –
у безденежного человека
голубые глаза.

Это не помогает.

Penniless Man

A penniless man
strolls about the streets.
Foggy stars tremble,
frost-bound.

Penniless man
is an armless man,
a legless man,
an eyeless man.

When all the city lights begin
to shine, everyone can clearly see
that the penniless man has got
blue eyes.

It doesn't help him.

* * *

Этот странный обычай
Присваивать людям имена
(или иногда номера)…
Без имени я уйду.
Без имени разве найдут.

Names

O that bizarre tradition
of giving people names
(or even numbers!)
Nameless, I will escape.
How can they possibly find
a nameless member of mankind?

Юрий Милорава
Yuri Milorava

Yuri Milorava was born in 1952 in Tbilisi, Georgia. A graduate of Tbilisi University for Foreign Languages, he lived in Moscow in the 1990s, and now is living in the USA. From the 1980s his poems appeared in émigré Russian and Ukrainian periodicals, e.g. in *The Continent, Chernovik* and *Khreschatyk,* and later in *The Anthology of Russian Vers Libre* (1991). He has published three collections of his poems, *Instead* (1996), *Distaff Angel* (2003) and *Ovejo* (2016), as well as his memoir about Viktor Shklovsky. He has also translated French and Georgian poetry into Russian.

* * *

единый
грубый дом на гребне
сожженья слой
из дыма
движущегося
несоразмерно

Untitled 1

a single
rugged house on the ridge
a burned layer shows
through the smoke
that moves
disproportionately

* * *

шоссе
со штабелями расколотых
не омытых
как малые дети в юдоли
и искореженных
глобальных
ликов

Untitled 2

a motorway
with stacks of cracked
unwashed
—like small children in the vale—
and twisted
global
faces

* * *

тайный винт
как розовая губчатость
цветы
внизу
повороты
шум
буйволы у воды
след угля и соли
множество стеклянных колонн

Untitled 3

a secret screw
like pink sponginess
flowers
down below
turns of the road
noise
buffaloes by the water
a trail of coal and salt
a multitude of glass columns

* * *

ввинчена
сдвинута
в монограмме упрека
в шуме
потаенная
весть-дверь

Untitled 4

screwed in
shifted
inside the monogram of reproach
amid the noise
a concealed
message-door

* * *

бытие
канатоходцев
и
тайная вечеря

Untitled 5

the life
of tight-rope walkers
their
last supper

Всеволод Некрасов
Vsevolod Nekrasov

Vsevolod Nekrasov (1934–2009) was born and lived in Moscow. He was a member of the now famous Lianozovo group of poets and painters. Under the Communists, he was a samizdat poet, without permission to publish his work openly. His poems appeared in unofficial Russian magazines, including *37*. Since 1989, three collections of his poetry, much appreciated, were published in Moscow. These books entitled *Poems from a Magazine* (1989), *Inquiry* (1991) and *Fair and Less than Fair* (1996) were followed by the Novosibirsk publication of his *Selected Poems* (2002) and *Poems 1956–1983* (Vologda, 2012). *Ein Deutsche Buch*, a book of his essays translated into German, appeared in Bochum in 2002. His poems have been translated into several other European languages.

* * *

Свобода есть
Свобода есть
Свобода есть
Свобода есть
Свобода есть
Свобода есть
Свобода есть свобода

Freedom

Freedom is
Freedom is
Freedom is
Freedom is
Freedom is
Freedom is
Freedom is freedom

* * *

Молчу
Молчи

Молчу
Молчи

Чутьем
Чутьем

Течем
Течем

Я думал
Мы о чем молчим

А мы молчали
Вот о чем

Untitled-1

I am silent
Keep silence

I am silent
Keep silence

By guess-work
By touch

We move on
We move further

I thought
We hushed something up

But we hushed up
This

* * *

надо же
и тишина между нами
мальчиками и девочками

кусты
столбы и луны
луны луны ну
не было войны

скажи ты

будто бы

а пусто было

не было
пусто

Untitled-2

picture this:
hushed silence dwells between us
between boys and girls

bushes
telegraph poles – and moons
many moons – as though
there was no war

one could say

as though
there was
only void

there wasn't

* * *

Стой

Чувствуй

Гордись

куда денешься

вот теперь и гордись

столица

и столица гордится

вечным памятником
великим нашим
начальникам

как они стучали
на нас

каким большим большим
Кулаком

Pride

Stop

Feel

Be proud

you have no place to hide

so be proud now

capital city –

our capital is proud too

of the eternal monuments
to our great leaders

how they banged
on their tables talking to us

banged on their tables with their big
BIG
Fists

* * *

Не люблю
Что я люблю
Но люблю
Что не люблю

Но что это я люблю
То что это я люблю
Это я не говорю
Что я это говорю

Love

I don't love
What I love
But I love
What I don't love

But what is it I love?
The fact that I love it
I am not saying
That I am saying that

Ры Никонова
Rea Nikonova

Rea Nikonova (pen name of Anna Tarshis, 1942–2014) was born in Sverdlovsk, lived for many years in Yeisk in southern Russia, and then in Kiel, Germany. She started writing poetry at the end of the 1950s, and later edited several samizdat magazines. Her rather experimental work was first published in samizdat and in the Western Russian-language magazines, before it began to appear in Russian periodicals in the 1990s. Her first collection of texts entitled *An Epigraph to Emptiness* was published in Moscow in 1997. She later had poetry books published in Germany, Canada and the U.S.A. *The Pared-Down Log of Poetry*, a volume of her new and collected poems, was published in 2002 in Spain. Gerald Janecek of Kentucky translated a number of her poems into English, and his translations have been widely anthologised. She won the Andrey Bely Poetry Prize and the David Burliuk Prize for life-long commitment to experimental poetry.

* * *

Кареты в белом
Портреты в черном
Все слуги в синем
все так красивы
все – из России
все так смешны
Все так нарошно
все так заброшено
    так огорожено
    так огорошено
Все так кошмарно
все так несложно

Simple

Ambulances in white
Portraits in black
All servants in blue
all are from Russia
all are so beautiful
all are so funny
Everything is so deliberate
everything is so abandoned
    so fenced off
    so uprooted
Everything is so eerie
everything is so simple

* * *

Все идиоты в этом мире идиотов
И каждый идиот идет отдельно

Все патриоты в этом мире идиотов
и каждый идиот идет отдельно

И каждый идиот по-каждому живет

В этом мире
в этом мире
каждый – идиот

The World of Idiots

How many idiots in this world of idiots
each idiot performing solo

How many patriots in this world of idiots
each idiot performing solo

And each idiot is an idiot in his own way

In this world
in this world
each one is an idiot

Анти-новелла

Полное отсутствие действия

Никто ничего не делает
Никто нигде не находится
Никто ни к чему не стремится

Финал
Апофеоз тишины

Anti-Novella

Absolute absence of action

No one does anything
No one is present anywhere
No one seeks after anything

The grand finale
Triumph of stillness

* * *

Когда помру
я стану знаменитой
Я знаменитой
знаменитой
стану
стану
Я стану
стану
стану
стану знаменитой
Ах
знаменитой
знаменитой
стану
стану

Foretaste

When I pop off
I shall be famous
Famous
famous
I shall be
I shall
I know
I shall
I shall
I shall be famous
Ah
how famous
famous
famous
I shall be

* * *

Россия с иссненным зубром!
Твоей заповедной золы
я запах храню
для неубранных
для сладостно помнящих дым

Russia

O Russia, with its snow-covered aurochs!
I keep the smell of your sacred ashes
for those unharvested
for those delighted to remember
the sweetest fumes

Генрих Сапгир
Genrikh Sapgir

Genrikh Sapgir (1928–1999) was born in Biysk, and lived in Moscow from his early childhood. He was a member of the now famous Lianozovo group of poets and painters. From 1959 he published poetry for children. As for his other poems, they only appeared in émigré magazines, such as *The Continent* and *Strelets / The Archer*. Since 1989 his poetry, short stories, plays and novels have been widely published in Russia. Three volumes of his *Collected Poems* appeared at the end of the 1990s. He represented Russia at numerous international festivals of poetry, and his work has been published in translation throughout the world. The English translations of his Psalms by Jim Kates of New Hampshire have been widely anthologised and highly appreciated. Sapgir was the recipient of various awards including the Pushkin Prize for poetry. He is regarded by many as the most important Russian poet of the second half of the twentieth century.

Роща

со всей своей зеленой тенью
с поросшими мохом голыми стволами
со всеми своими гладкими листочками и птицами
со всеми своими ползающими и бегающими
с грузином который порвал газету
и приспустив штаны сидит на корточках
быть может вся эта самшитовая роща –
одна вечно-зеленая трель соловья

Grove

with all its green shadows
with naked tree boles covered with moss
with all its birds and smooth leaves
with all that creep and run
with a Georgian man who has just torn a newspaper
lowered his pants and squatted down –
perhaps this boxwood grove is
an evergreen trill of a nightingale

* * *

Говорили
И тут солнышко светит
Говорили
И тут люди живут
Не верю
Третий день ни с кем не заговариваю
Боюсь
Вдруг не ответит

New in Town

I was told
The sun shines here too
I was told
People live here too
I do not believe it
For three days I haven't spoken to anyone
I'm afraid
They won't respond

* * *

Красные портьеры
Розовые стены
Голубая комбинация
И комбинация
Из этих цветов
И я готов
Уже готов
Жить
Тут
Любить
Здесь
Сплавлять
Лес
И удивлять
Простых людей
Наличием
Простых идей

Business Trip

Red curtains
Pink walls
Blue underwear
And the combination
Of these colours
I'm ready now
Ready
To live
Here
To fall in love
Here
To raft
Wood
And to surprise
Simple people
With my
Simple ideas

Изречение

Человек не должен забывать
Что у него есть зад
И просто обязан помнить
Что у него есть крылья

A Proverb

Man mustn't forget
That he has a backside
And just ought to remember
That he has wings

* * *

Тс-с
Слышите

И еще

И это

И там

И далеко-далеко

Sounds of Silence

Hark, hearer
can you hear it?

And this

And again

And there

And far, far away

Ян Сатуновский
Ian Satunovsky

Ian Satunovsky (pen name of Yakov Satunovsky, 1913–1982) was born in Dnipro, Ukraine, and moved to Moscow as a teenager to study in a college. In 1931 he returned to Dnipro to study physical chemistry at Dnepropetrovsk State University, from which he graduated in 1938. He served in the Russian army from 1939 until the end of World War II. Having come back from the war, he settled in Electrostal near Moscow, where he worked as an engineer. He was close to the poets of the Lianozovo Group, and published fourteen books of his poetry for children. From the mid-1970s he published his poetic miniatures in émigré magazines. He printed seven copies of his *Selected Poems* on his home typewriter; they were bound as three volumes. Four critically acclaimed collections of his poems were published in Moscow posthumously, the latest being *Poems and Prose to Go with Them* (2012).

* * *

В век сплошной электрификации
всем
всё
до лампочки.
Так что даже левые поэты
пишут
правые стихи.

Changing the Bulb

In the age
of total electrification
no one
cares a damn.
And so left-wing poets
write
right-wing poems.

* * *

Экспрессионизм-сионизм.
Импрессионизм-сионизм.
Но и в РЕАЛИЗМЕ, при желании,
обнаружат сговор с ИЗРАИЛЕМ.

If They So Desire

Expressionism is Zionism.
Impressionism is Zionism.
But even in REALISM, if they so desire,
they will discover a collusion with ISRAEL.

* * *

Ребенок рисунка:
вроде как машинально,
почти по ошибке
художник
нанес на холст
смертельный намек.

Almost by Mistake

A child of the drawing:
seemingly in a mechanical way,
almost by mistake
the artist
deposited a deadly allusion
onto the canvas.

* * *

...а, впрочем,
не всё ли нам равно – писать – свободным
или каким-нибудь еще – стихом
в концентрационном лагере...

Writing

                                             ... but then
isn't it all the same to us – to write in free verse
or in some other kind of verse
in this concentration camp...

* * *

Я Мойша з Бердычева.
      Я Мо́йзбер.
А, может быть, Райзман.
        Гинцбург, может быть.
Я плюнул в лицо
      оккупантским гадинам.
Меня закопали в глину заживо.
Я Вайнберг.
Я Вайнберг из Пятихатки.
Я Вайнберг.
     За что меня расстреляли?
Я жид пархатый дерьмом напхатый.
Мне памятник стоит в Роттердаме.

A Bloody Yid

I am Moishe from Berdichiv.
                      I'm Moisber.
Or maybe Raizman.
                      Perhaps Ginsburg.
I spat in the faces
              of the invading scum.
I was buried alive in clay.
I'm Weinberg.
I'm Weinberg from Pyatikhatka.
I'm Weinberg.
          Why did they shoot me?
I'm a bloody yid stuffed with shit.
A monument to me was erected in Rotterdam.

Ася Шнейдерман
Asya Shneiderman

Asya Shneiderman was born in 1968 in St. Petersburg, the only daughter of the well-known Russian painter and sculptor Liubov Dobashina. After studying English and art at Herzen University, St. Petersburg, she worked as a teacher of English, and now works as a librarian. Since the end of 1990s her poems and short stories have been published in various Russian magazines and anthologies. Her first book of poems entitled *Marking Silence with a Word* was published in Moscow in 1998; her second, *The Other*, in Saint-Petersburg in 2007. Her translations from the Irish poet Desmond Egan appeared in his bilingual English/Russian *Selected Poems*.

* * *

Не писать стихи, а слышать,
и с прилежностью стенографистки,
не пропуская ни звука, ни знака, –
без помарок строчить.
Повтор невозможен.
Душа
похожа на узкую длинную реку.

Poetry

Not to write poetry,
but to hear it
and to scribble without slips of the pen,
with the diligence of a stenographer,
not missing a sound or a sign.
Repetition is impossible.
Soul
resembles a narrow long river.

* * *

Разве башня из камня
властна над ветром,
поселившимся в ней?
Это он колышет ее изнутри,
очертанья меняет.
Так и тело.
Так и душа.

The Tower

Does this stone tower
have power over the wind
dwelling therein?
No, it is the wind that sways it from inside
and changes its shape.

Behold, the soul –
and its bodily stronghold.

* * *

Город влажный лежал под нами –
купола раскрытых зонтов, закрытых, шпили –
куполов бокалы, шпилей фужеры –
мужчина и женщина –
вожделенный, желанный город.
Только крыши тонкая жесть,
только боль
между нами,
между нами и небом.

The City

The damp city rests beneath us –
domed umbrellas, spear-shaped umbrellas,
broach-spires, cup-like domes, goblet-like domes.
A man and a woman –
and a city,
the desired, beloved city.
Between us
only the thin tin plates of this roof
and the pain.
Only the pain between you and me.
Between the two of us and the sky.

* * *

Лене Жуковой

Друзья приходят в наш дом
и, точно двери балкона,
где пьют кофе и курят,
раскрывают нам свои жизни.

На пороге балкона стою,
смотрю на этих людей
сквозь дыма завесу и сквозь
тростниковую занавеску.

…Ничего не знать об их жизни.
Только догадываться.

Poem for Lena Zhukova

Friends come to our house
and, like the balcony door,
reveal their lives to us.
The balcony where they drink coffee and smoke…

I stand on its threshold,
and look at these people
through the veil of smoke and
the reed curtain.

…Not to know a thing about their lives.
Only to guess.

* * *

Особенно в мире,
где окончательно и бесповоротно,
везде и во всем,
слева и справа,
сверху и снизу
изо всех возможных
строев, религий, учений
побеждает цинизм, –
не фокус
в своей отдельно
взятой жизни
быть целенаправленным
циником.

Диссидентство,
безумство,
salto mortale –
любить.

Especially in this Kind of World

Especially in this kind of world
where definitively and irrevocably,
everywhere and in everything,
to the left and to the right,
high up and down below,
of all possible
regimes, religions and teachings
the one that wins is cynicism,
you need no tricks
in your personal life,
in this particular life of yours,
to become an accomplished
cynic.

To be in love
is dissent,
madness,
a *salto mortale*.

Михаил Соковнин
Mikhail Sokovnin

Mikhail Sokovnin (1938–1975) was born and lived in Moscow. A graduate of the Russian Literature Department of Moscow State Pedagogical University, he worked as a tour-guide in a number of Moscow art museums. His poems, prose and translations from Alfred Tennison weren't published during his lifetime. The first posthumous publication occurred in 1978 in Paris. In the 1990s his poems began to appear in Russian periodicals. His first posthumous collection, *Discomposed Type,* appeared in 1995; his second, *Prose and Poetry,* in 2012.

* * *

Вот вам и чудо:
из голубого пруда
торчит чертик.
Да,
на фантазию всюду
и всегда
нужна зацепка.
В данном случае –
щепка.

Fantasy

Here's a miracle for you:
a little devil
sticks out of the blue pond.
Yes,
to get fantasy
up and running
one always needs a lever.
In this case,
a sliver.

Лесовик

Н.С.Г.

Лесовик уставился на – солнце.
Будто понимает, что оно –
что оно с собою унесется
даже в землю, где всегда темно,
и что если не забудет солнца,
по закону солнца-колеса
он опять родится, как проснется,
и продлится
сон лесовика.

Woodsman

For N. S. G.

The woodsman stares at the sun –
As though he just realised that it –
That it will be carried away, by itself,
Even as far as the land of constant darkness,
And also that, if he doesn't forget the sun,
he'll be born again as he wakes up
according to the law of the sun-wheel –
and the woodsman's dream
will linger.

* * *

Самовар.
Сеновал.
Лето перезимовал.
Осень – ветер,
осень – дождь...
Так и смерть переживешь.

Samovar

A samovar.
A hayloft.
…hibernated the whole summer.
Autumn is wind,
autumn is rain.
This way you'll survive your death.

* * *

Небо серое-серое.
Небо северное.
Мало перьев на сосне,
и сквозящая макушка
в небо просится.
Отчего она, кукушка,
по весне?
Отчего она не по осени?

A Northern Song

The sky is the greyest grey.
The sky is a northern one.
There're some feathers atop the pine,
and its drafty crown
strives for the sky.
Why is this cuckoo
in spring?
Why isn't it in autumn?

* * *

Заброшенные истины,
колодцы прежних дней.
Над травами когтистыми
пустые перстни пней.

Untitled

Abandoned truths,
wells from the days of old...
Above the clawed grass,
empty signet rings of stumps.

Сергей Стратановский
Sergey Stratanovsky

Sergey Stratanovsky was born in 1944 in St. Petersburg. Having studied philology at St. Petersburg University, he has since worked as a librarian. He started writing poetry at the end of the 1960s; his poems have first been published in samizdat and in some Western Russian-language magazines. He belonged to the so-called New Leningrad school of poetry, which also included Joseph Brodsky, Elena Shvarts and Viktor Krivulin. His first collection entitled simply *Poems* was published in St. Petersburg in 1993. Nine critically acclaimed books of his poems followed more recently, the latest being *Dissonant Polyphony* (2016). Stratanovsky is regarded by many as one of the most prominent St. Petersburg poets of his generation.

* * *

Ночью, в Набоков-отеле
        школьницу, полую Лолу
В номер на птицу-постель
        змей-господин завлечет
Змей о семи головах:
        первая жрет насекомых
Гонгорой бредит вторая
Третья целует в пупок,
        в полудетские груди Лолиту
Зверь о семи головах
Веки закрыла седьмая:
        молится Богу впотьмах

In the Nabokov Hotel

At night, in the Nabokov Hotel
Sir Serpent entices a school-girl,
    the hollow Lola, into his room
    and onto his bird-shaped bed.
Seven-headed Sir Serpent.
The first head gorges itself on insects,
The second is mad about Gongora,
The third kisses Lolita on her navel
    and childish breasts.
Seven-headed Sir Beast.
The last head has weighed its eyelids down
    to pray to some God in the dark.

Акула-кунсткамера

Вот акула-кунсткамера. В ней
Головы турок в спирту
Петр в железных ботфортах
Церберша ангальт-цербстская:
   в ноздрях сияют алмазы
В заднице блещет топаз
Рядом кленовый Пахом,
   ладан, церковное пенье
Пушкин на девке верхом,
   пишущий стихотворенье
Дивно бродить и смотреть
В многокамерной рыбе, правдивой как смерть

A Shark as a Cabinet of Curiosities

A Shark as a Cabinet of Curiosities
Inside a shark there is a Cabinet of Curiosities.
Watch these heads of Turks preserved
      in alcohol, Tzar Peter in his iron jackboots,
The Cerberus of Anhalt-Zerbst,
      diamonds shining in her nostrils
And a topaz sparkling in her ass-hole.
The maple Pakhom sits beside her.
It smells of an incense, a choir is singing.
Pushkin is also there positioned on top
      of a whore and writing a poem.
I do like to stroll through these rooms
      looking round and holding my breath
In this spacious fish, truthful as death.

Левиафан

Чешуеглазый,
      с дрожащим Ионой во чреве
В недрах узилища рыбного,
      в тесноте кровокамеры хищной
Страшно и нечем дышать
      в государстве его биоклеток
В социуме телец
      кровяных
            под командой турбинного мозга
Скоро ль извергнешь назад
      поглощенных, заглоченных толпы?
Скоро ль нырнешь без возврата
      вниз, на библейское дно?

Leviathan

Scaly-eyed,
  it harbours trembling Jonah in its belly,
In the bowels of its fishy dungeon.
How scary it must be –
  choking in that cramped
Blood-coloured chamber
  of some predatory cellulate republic,
Suffocating in the community of blood corpuscles
  under the command of a turbine brain!

When will you disgorge what you have swallowed,
  those countless multitudes?
When will you dive back
  to the scriptural depths, forever?

Башня-библиотека

Башня до самого неба,
        башня-библиотека
Вьющихся лестниц извивы,
        фолианты в размер этажей
Хмель-виноградьем увитые
        с заржавленными замками
На шумерских цепях
Здесь чернокнижье цветущее –
        тайную мудрость Адама
Кто-то постигнет, вместит,
        и тогда остановится время
Ангел свернет небеса

The Library Tower

It's a library tower,
      and it pierces the sky.
Hop and vine twine around
Winding stairs and storey-sized volumes.
All the locks on Sumerian chains
      are rusting.
Black magic is blooming here,
      the secret wisdom of Adam.
Some day somebody will apprehend
      and master it –
And time will come to a halt,
An angel will furl the sky

Апокриф

Вирус, откуда-то появившийся
И в Адама вселившийся
            на террасе Эдемского сада
Вирус, боль вызывающий,
Сокрушающий чресла,
            кровь рушащий,
Вирус невидимый
И Адам пораженный
            уходит из райского сада
Сам уходит,
            на горькую землю труда

An Apocryphal Story

The virus that appeared from Goodness knows where
And made its home inside Adam
        on the terrace of the Garden of Eden –
The virus causing pain,
Crushing the loins,
        ruining the blood,
The invisible virus –
And Adam, staggering,
        leaves the wonders of Eden,
Of his own will descends he
        onto the bitter earth of Labour

Аркадий Тюрин
Arkady Tyurin

Arkady Tyurin (1952–1996) lived in Moscow. He graduated from Gorky Literary Institute, and later worked as an editor for the Sovetsky Pisatel Publishing House. Tyurin began writing poetry in the 1970s but only achieved a certain degree of recognition in the 1980s and '90s when a few anthologies of Russian free verse poetry were published, *White Square* (1988), *Time X* (1989) and *The Anthology of Russian Vers Libre* (1991). He published two collections of his poems titled *I Have Seen* (1988) and *The Colour of the Earth* (1989), and later a joint collection titled *White Square Two* (with Karen Dzhangirov, in 1992). Two of his short stories appeared in literary periodicals. His poems were also published in translation into Bulgarian.

Неразрывность

Пока истины упакованы в слова
Вся правда мира
Умещается в одном
Слове с ложью,
И самый гениальный мистификатор
Не сумеет отколоть
Кусочек чистой,
Без примеси,
Лжи.

Inseparability

As long as truths are packed into words,
The whole truth of the world
Fits into a word
Together with a lie.
And even the most ingenious wonder-worker
Won't be able to break off
A morsel of pure
Unadulterated
Lie.

Неосторожно...

Сны толковать
И предсказывать раны,
Мысли читать –
Неосторожно...
Знать о других
И не знать о себе,
Изнывать от предчувствий,
Лица в толпе узнавать,
Вечером шорохи
Слышать за дверью,
Неосторожно
Видеть в изломе ветвей
Странные знаки
Судьбы.

It Is Careless of You ...

To interpret dreams
And to predict wounds,
To read thoughts
Inadvertently...
To know things about others
And not to know much about yourself,
To be weary of forebodings,
To recognise people in the crowd,
To hear rustling in the evening
Outside the door,
To see heedlessly some
Strange signs of fate
In the pattern
Of broken branches.

* * *

Все отражает, не унося,
Река. А время
Все уносит, ничего не отразив.

Time and the River

The river reflects all
Without taking it away.
But time takes all away
Without reflecting anything.

* * *

Был ей другом.
Ушла
Искать хозяина.

She

I was her friend.
She left me
To look for an owner.

* * *

Запущен
Сад жизни;
Глаза мои
Заросли окнами,
Окна заросли
Стёклами,
Стекла заросли
Небом,
Небо заросло
Звездами.
Звезды заросли светом,
Но свет зарос тьмой.
Запущен сад жизни:
В нем не было бы видно
Ничего,
Если бы тьма
Не заросла
Глазами.

Garden

The garden of life
Is unkempt;
My eyes
Are overgrown with windows,
The windows overgrown
With glass,
The panes overgrown
With the sky,
The sky overgrown
With stars.
The stars are overgrown with light,
But the light is overgrown with darkness.
The garden of life is unkempt:
We wouldn't be able to see
Anything,
If the darkness
Wasn't overgrown
With eyes.

Алина Витухновская
Alina Vitukhnovskaya

Alina Vitukhnovskaya was born in 1973 in Moscow, and from her youth worked as a journalist. Having started writing poetry in the late 1980s, she published several collections of her poems, including *Anomalism* (1993), *The Children's Book of the Dead* (1994), *A Romance with Fenamin* (1999) and *Pre-Being* (2015). In 1990, the Russian authorities imprisoned her – allegedly for drug dealing, but, according to newspaper reports, for a refusal to become a FSB/KGB informer. At that time she had the support of most of the Russian intellectuals who protested against her unjust imprisonment and campaigned for her release. A book of her selected poems in German translation entitled *Schwarze Ikone* was published in Germany in 2002. She is regarded by many as one of the strongest "protest" voices in contemporary Russia, and is currently the coordinator of the Republican Alternative political movement.

На ощупь

Она воспринимала
Как бы на ощупь,
Всерьез
Какой-нибудь
Мороженный там хек,
Бананы, спички –
«Сие подорожало
В связи с войной» –
Заметила она.
Вот сколько ни живи – сего мне не узнать
(Познать).
Почувствовать – тем более, мне не...

А что война мне?
Я с рожденья на войне.

By Touch

She perceived
As if by touch,
Pensively,
Some
Frozen hake,
Bananas, matches.
"They all went up in price
Because of the war,"
She made a remark.
No matter how long I'll live, I'll never
Understand (or perceive)
Or feel – more so, since I'm not...

And what is war to me?
From birth I am inside the war.

Ваш хаос

Вам хаос-оса,
Ей «Ха!» —
Скажите, усмехаясь.
Вам кажется,
Что нет хаоса,
А есть трость.

Your Chaos

For you, chaos is a wasp,
But she says "Ha!"
With a grin.
Don't you think
That there's no chaos,
Just a stick?

Ноль

Ноль,
Вычерпавший
Нутро себя.
Луна скользит как краб.
Нежен раб оливковый,
Фруктами кормимый.
Ничтожество его
Люблю любить
Я –
Ноль,
Вычерпавший
Нутро себя.

Zero

A Zero
That gutted
Itself.
The moon glides like a crab.
The olive slave fed with exotic fruit
Is tender.
I love to love
His nothingness;
I am
A Zero
That gutted
Itself.

Собака Павлова

Считалось, что нужно
вымыть руки, вытереть
махровым полотенцем, закончить
школу, различать
мужчину и женщину, основные направления
современной
философии,
вести учет
бумагам, ежегодно
обследоваться в районной
поликлинике,
похоронить мать, дерево вырастить, сына
считаться отцом,
знать уголовный кодекс, врага в лицо –
зачем? Если можно стрелять ему в спину.

Pavlov's Dog

They say, one must
wash his hands and then dry them
with a Turkish towel, go to school,
be able to tell a man from a woman,
be acquainted with popular trends
in modern philosophy,
register incoming papers,
have regular check-ups
at the local doctor's,
bury his mother, plant a tree,
be regarded as his son's father,
know the criminal code,
know his enemy by sight –
but what for? One may just as well
shoot him in the back.

Ева Браунинг

Где ты
Ева Браунинг
мглистая девочка зверств
Лолиточка пистолетов
ласковых оккупаций

корявая куколка смерти
муза расовых чисток
пациентка конца
любовница абсолюта

Где ты
Ева Браунинг
мудрая бабочка Вагнера
муть арийского хаоса
Русская мать насилия?

Eva Browning

Where are you
Eva Browning
brutality's misty girl
Little Lolita of pistols
and tender annexations

crooked chrysalis of death
Muse of ethnic cleansing
private patient
of The End
concubine of the absolute?

Where are you
Eva Browning
Wagner's wise butterfly
residue of Aryan chaos
the mother of Russian violence?

Acropolis – The Wawel Plays
by Stanisław Wyspiański

Stanisław Wyspiański (1869-1907) achieved worldwide fame, both as a painter, and Poland's greatest dramatist of the first half of the twentieth century. *Acropolis: the Wawel Plays*, brings together four of Wyspiański's most important dramatic works in a new English translation by Charles S. Kraszewski. All of the plays centre on Wawel Hill: the legendary seat of royal and ecclesiastical power in the poet's native city, the ancient capital of Poland. In these plays, Wyspiański explores the foundational myths of his nation: that of the self-sacrificial Wanda, and the struggle between King Bolesław the Bold and Bishop Stanisław Szczepanowski. In the eponymous play which brings the cycle to an end, Wyspiański carefully considers the value of myth to a nation without political autonomy, soaring in thought into an apocalyptic vision of the future. Richly illustrated with the poet's artwork, *Acropolis: the Wawel Plays* also contains Wyspiański's architectural proposal for the renovation of Wawel Hill, and a detailed critical introduction by the translator. In its plaited presentation of *Bolesław the Bold* and *Skałka*, the translation offers, for the first time, the two plays in the unified, composite format that the poet intended, but was prevented from carrying out by his untimely death.

Buy it > www.glagoslav.com

Contours of the City
by Attyla Mohylny

Contours of the City arguably comprises one of the finest collections of free verse ever written in Ukrainian even though it was largely overlooked when it first appeared during the political transition to Ukrainian independence in 1991. It certainly deserves a broader audience both in Mohylny's homeland as well as in the wider world. While it may be described as a one-hit wonder because of the poet's premature death, it remains a brilliant hit for all time.

Translator Michael Naydan received the Eugene Kayden Meritorious Achievement Award in Translation from the University of Colorado for a partial manuscript of his translations of Mohylny's poetry into English in 1993. This edition includes a complete translation of Mohylny's collection *Contours of the City* along with several poems translated by Virlana Tkacz and Wanda Phipps.

Buy it > www.glagoslav.com

TIME OF THE OCTOPUS

by Anatoly Kucherena

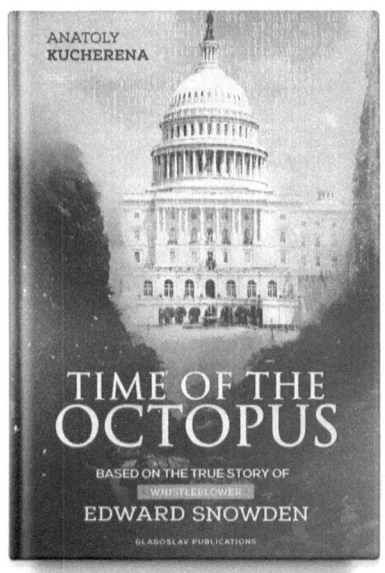

A frightening, prophetic vision of our world...
In Moscow's Sheremetyevo airport, fugitive US intelligence officer Joshua Kold is held in limbo, unable to leave the airport's transit area. He is on the run, after blowing the lid off the terrifying reach of covert American global surveillance operations. Will the Russian authorities grant him asylum, or will they hand him over the clutches of the global octopus eager for revenge for his betrayal?
As this gripping psychological and political thriller unfolds, a Moscow lawyer takes Kold to a secret bunker and grills him intently on just why he did it. Upon Kold's answers hang not only his own fate, but much, much more as the true extent of this chilling 1984 world unfolds.
Anatoly Kucherena is the famous Russian lawyer who took on the case of the American whistleblower Edward Snowden whose revelations about US intelligence operations sent shockwaves around the world in 2013. Time of the Octopus is a fiction, but it is based on Kucherena's own interviews with Snowden at Sheremetyevo, and provides the basis for Oliver Stone's major Hollywood movie 'Snowden' starring Joseph Gordon-Levitt, one of the movie events of 2016...

Buy it > www.glagoslav.com

The Frontier
28 Contemporary Ukrainian Poets - An Anthology

This anthology reflects a search of the Ukrainian nation for its identity, the roots of which lie deep inside Ukrainian-language poetry. Some of the included poets are well-known locally and internationally; among them are Serhiy Zhadan, Halyna Kruk, Ostap Slyvynsky, Marianna Kijanowska, Oleh Kotsarev, Anna Bagriana and, of course, the living legend of Ukrainian poetry, Vasyl Holoborodko. The next Ukrainian poetic generation also features prominently in the collection. Such poets as Les Beley, Olena Herasymyuk, Myroslav Laiuk, Hanna Malihon, Taras Malkovych, Julia Musakovska, Julia Stahivska and Lyuba Yakimchuk are the ones Ukrainians like to read today, and each of them already has an excellent reputation abroad due to festival appearances and translations to European languages. The work collected here documents poetry in Ukraine responding to challenges of the time by forging a radical new poetic, reconsidering writing techniques and language itself.

Edited and translated from the Ukrainian by Anatoly Kudryavitsky.

A Bilingual Edition.

Buy it > www.glagoslav.com

The Grand Harmony
by Bohdan Ihor Antonych

The extraordinarily inventive Ukrainian poet and literary critic Bohdan Ihor Antonych (1909-1937), the son of a Catholic priest, died prematurely at the early age of 28 of pneumonia. Originally from the mountainous Lemko region in Poland, where a variant of Ukrainian is spoken, he was home-schooled for the first eleven years of his life because of frequent illness. He began to write poetry in Ukrainian after he moved to the Western Ukrainian city of Lviv to continue his studies at the University of Lviv.

A collection of poems on religious themes written in 1932 and 1933, *The Grand Harmony* is a subtle and supple examination of Antonych's intimately personal journey to faith, with all its revelatory verities as well as self-questioning and doubt. The collection marks the beginning of Antonych's development into one of the greatest poets of his time.

Buy it > www.glagoslav.com

Dear Reader,

Thank you for purchasing this book.

We at Glagoslav Publications are glad to welcome you, and hope that you find our books to be a source of knowledge and inspiration.

We want to show the beauty and depth of the Slavic region to everyone looking to expand their horizon and learn something new about different cultures, different people, and we believe that with this book we have managed to do just that.

Now that you've got to know us, we want to get to know you. We value communication with our readers and want to hear from you! We offer several options:

– Join our Book Club on Goodreads, Library Thing and Shelfari, and receive special offers and information about our giveaways;

– Share your opinion about our books on Amazon, Barnes & Noble, Waterstones and other bookstores;

– Join us on Facebook and Instagram for updates on our publications and news about our authors;

– Visit our site www.glagoslav.com to check out our Catalogue and subscribe to our Newsletter.

Glagoslav Publications is getting ready to release a new collection and planning some interesting surprises — stay with us to find out!

Glagoslav Publications B.V.
Ringbaan Oost 102
5013 CD Tilburg
The Netherlands
Tel.: + 31 (0) 13 369 95 74
Email: contact@glagoslav.com

Glagoslav Publications Catalogue

- *The Time of Women* by Elena Chizhova
- *Andrei Tarkovsky: The Collector of Dreams* by Layla Alexander-Garrett
- *Andrei Tarkovsky - A Life on the Cross* by Lyudmila Boyadzhieva
- *Sin* by Zakhar Prilepin
- *Hardly Ever Otherwise* by Maria Matios
- *Khatyn* by Ales Adamovich
- *The Lost Button* by Irene Rozdobudko
- *Christened with Crosses* by Eduard Kochergin
- *The Vital Needs of the Dead* by Igor Sakhnovsky
- *The Sarabande of Sara's Band* by Larysa Denysenko
- *A Poet and Bin Laden* by Hamid Ismailov
- *Watching The Russians (Dutch Edition)* by Maria Konyukova
- *Kobzar* by Taras Shevchenko
- *The Stone Bridge* by Alexander Terekhov
- *Moryak* by Lee Mandel
- *King Stakh's Wild Hunt* by Uladzimir Karatkevich
- *The Hawks of Peace* by Dmitry Rogozin
- *Harlequin's Costume* by Leonid Yuzefovich
- *Depeche Mode* by Serhii Zhadan
- *The Grand Slam and other stories (Dutch Edition)* by Leonid Andreev
- *METRO 2033 (Dutch Edition)* by Dmitry Glukhovsky
- *METRO 2034 (Dutch Edition)* by Dmitry Glukhovsky
- *A Russian Story* by Eugenia Kononenko
- *Herstories, An Anthology of New Ukrainian Women Prose Writers*
- *The Battle of the Sexes Russian Style* by Nadezhda Ptushkina
- *A Book Without Photographs* by Sergey Shargunov
- *Down Among The Fishes* by Natalka Babina
- *disUNITY* by Anatoly Kudryavitsky
- *Sankya* by Zakhar Prilepin
- *Wolf Messing* by Tatiana Lungin
- *Good Stalin* by Victor Erofeyev

- *Solar Plexus* by Rustam Ibragimbekov
- *Don't Call me a Victim!* by Dina Yafasova
- *Poetin (Dutch Edition)* by Chris Hutchins and Alexander Korobko
- *A History of Belarus* by Lubov Bazan
- *Children's Fashion of the Russian Empire* by Alexander Vasiliev
- *Empire of Corruption - The Russian National Pastime* by Vladimir Soloviev
- *Heroes of the 90s - People and Money. The Modern History of Russian Capitalism*
- *Fifty Highlights from the Russian Literature (Dutch Edition)* by Maarten Tengbergen
- *Bajesvolk (Dutch Edition)* by Mikhail Khodorkovsky
- *Tsarina Alexandra's Diary (Dutch Edition)*
- *Myths about Russia* by Vladimir Medinskiy
- *Boris Yeltsin - The Decade that Shook the World* by Boris Minaev
- *A Man Of Change - A study of the political life of Boris Yeltsin*
- *Sberbank - The Rebirth of Russia's Financial Giant* by Evgeny Karasyuk
- *To Get Ukraine* by Oleksandr Shyshko
- *Asystole* by Oleg Pavlov
- *Gnedich* by Maria Rybakova
- *Marina Tsvetaeva - The Essential Poetry*
- *Multiple Personalities* by Tatyana Shcherbina
- *The Investigator* by Margarita Khemlin
- *The Exile* by Zinaida Tulub
- *Leo Tolstoy – Flight from paradise* by Pavel Basinsky
- *Moscow in the 1930* by Natalia Gromova
- *Laurus (Dutch edition)* by Evgenij Vodolazkin
- *Prisoner* by Anna Nemzer
- *The Crime of Chernobyl - The Nuclear Goulag* by Wladimir Tchertkoff
- *Alpine Ballad* by Vasil Bykau
- *The Complete Correspondence of Hryhory Skovoroda*

- *The Tale of Aypi* by Ak Welsapar
- *Selected Poems* by Lydia Grigorieva
- *The Fantastic Worlds of Yuri Vynnychuk*
- *The Garden of Divine Songs and Collected Poetry of Hryhory Skovoroda*
- *Adventures in the Slavic Kitchen: A Book of Essays with Recipes*
- *Seven Signs of the Lion* by Michael M. Naydan
- *Forefathers' Eve* by Adam Mickiewicz
- *One-Two* by Igor Eliseev
- *Girls, be Good* by Bojan Babić
- *Time of the Octopus* by Anatoly Kucherena
- *Soghomon Tehlirian Memories - The Assassination of Talaat*
- *The Grand Harmony* by Bohdan Ihor Antonych
- *The Selected Lyric Poetry Of Maksym Rylsky*
- *The Shining Light* by Galymkair Mutanov
- *The Frontier: 28 Contemporary Ukrainian Poets - An Anthology*
- *Acropolis - The Wawel Plays* by Stanisław Wyspiański
- *Contours of the City* by Attyla Mohylny
- *Conversations Before Silence: The Selected Poetry of Oles Ilchenko*
- *Nikolai Gumilev's Africa*
- *Zinnober's Poppets* by Elena Chizhova
- *The Hemingway Game* by Evgeni Grishkovets

More coming soon...

www.ingramcontent.com/pod-product-compliance
Lightning Source LLC
Chambersburg PA
CBHW031055080526
44587CB00011B/686